Advance P.

Women of Scar Clan

Lynne Klippel's *Women of Scar Clan: True Stories of Transcendence* is an engrossing read that speaks to the soul and guides each of us through our own personal journey to obtain a deeper understanding of ourselves and our experiences. Each experience and journey is different, yet consistently authentic, heartfelt, and genuine.

Klippel does an amazing job of illustrating the differences and similarities between feminine experiences so as to emphasize and honor each individual's evolution. Klippel's use of *Woman of Scar Clan* to reach readers in need of healing where they are is commendable and a much-needed option for those seeking guidance and understanding. Across demographics, individuals will quickly come to appreciate the diverse narrations in this work. The way Klippel engages this sensitive subject matter is breathtaking. This work will speak into your life again and again over the years to come.

~Manhattan Book Review

There are plenty of inspirational memoirs on the market, but *Women of Scar Clan* adds a layer of inspection into not just the roots of pain, but its potential for transformation. The mechanics of this process receive close inspection with an eye to showing how pain, anger, and angst can be translated into positive avenues of change. The lessons that stem from individual experience and move into cultural and social change create an inspirational guide that doesn't just invite but demands 'looking in the mirror' in order to be effective. This approach is highly recommended for women considering transformative experiences and their opportunities. It invites them to contribute to a better world and choose wisely, with the goal of making a difference.

There should be more books like *Women of Scar Clan* on the market today: accessible, wide-ranging, and connecting personal experience to social inspection and improvement. The world would be a better place if these lessons were absorbed early in life.

~D. Donovan, Senior Reviewer, Midwest Book Review

A volume of true stories and motivational quotes features women who have succeeded after overcoming obstacles. The women described in the book have endured illnesses, abuse, family separation, and other issues, only to come out stronger on the other side. The author, who interviewed over 100 women for this work, also shares her own experience of following her dream to lead a simpler life in Ecuador. The subjects of Klippel's tales are diverse and intriguing, particularly her daughter-in-law, Allie, a chemist who speaks about the importance of experiencing failure in both her profession and her personal life. This heartfelt, inspirational collection that focuses on remarkable women will comfort.

~Kirkus Reviews

"A heartwarming book that speaks to your soul in a deep, authentic manner that will leave readers eager for more. For those who have grown up reading the *Chicken Soup For The Soul* series, this is right up your alley. Readers will find comfort and joy between the pages. Have your box of tissues ready and let the healing begin."

~ San Francisco Book Review

Women of Scar Clan
True Stories of Transcendence

Lynne Klippel

THOMAS NOBLE BOOKS

Author Contact: WomenofScarClan.com, LynneKlippel.com

Thomas Noble Books

427 N Tatnall #90947

Wilmington, DE 19801

ISBN: 978-1-945586-23-1

Library of Congress Control Number:2019917040

First Printing: 2019

ı

This book is for my granddaughter, Lucy, and her amazing mother, Allie. Thank you both for the joy you've brought to my life.

TABLE OF CONTENTS

Section 4

Section 5

Section 6

Section 7

Section 8

"Now, every time I witness a strong person, I want to know: What dark did you conquer in your story? Mountains do not rise without earthquakes."

- Katherine MacKennett

Dear Reader

Come sit by my fire and let me tell you some stories.

These are true stories, lived by women who might be your sisters, co-workers or neighbors. They are not about pain, but about transcendence, and they are preserved in this book because they are important. They point to the power of courage and intuition, and to the stubborn commitment to getting up and trying again, even after failure, abuse, or injury.

Three years ago, I learned I was going to become a grandmother. When I found out that the baby was a little girl, I was overjoyed. But I also started to think about how cruel life can be. I'm an older grandmother, so I knew that by the time my granddaughter was an adult, and life was beating her up, there was a chance that I wouldn't be around to encourage and support her.

I decided to start collecting empowering stories, and the idea snowballed into something bigger and more powerful than even I could have imagined. I ended up interviewing more than one hundred women, and in my journey, I sought diversity by interviewing women of many races, creeds, and socioeconomic groups. They ranged in age from sixteen to ninety-four and lived on four different continents. Some of the interviews took place in fine homes, others in cinder block houses with dirt floors, while many were conducted via Skype. Each interview was a gift and taught me something valuable.

Over time, I began to see a pattern in the stories. All of the women had been wounded by something. One woman lost her home and her freedom due to war, while other women lost children, body parts, their health, security, or their innocence and confidence from horrendous abuse. Some women were harmed because of who they loved or what they believed, and others made mistakes that caused them deep pain. Some risked everything to follow their heart, losing the comfort of home and familiarity, and while the wounds were universal, the responses to those wounds differed.

The Department of Environment and Conservation in New South Wales, Australia, studied tree scars. These scars provide important clues as to the activities of both Aboriginal peoples and early settlers in Australia. In the days before hardware stores and lumber yards, tree bark was stripped and used for shelters, canoes, shields, twine, fishing line, and many other things. Aboriginal people also carved scars into trees for communication and ceremonial purposes. In Australia, scarred trees are now protected as a part of Aboriginal Heritage, because they mark places where important events occurred.

These studies found that softwood trees, such as eucalyptus, can become hollow and weak after bark stripping, while hardwood trees had the best recovery. What they also found out was that there are four potential outcomes after a tree is scarred:

- **Dieback**- Trees continue to lose bark after the first cut. Insects or moisture gets into the heart of the tree and it dies from the injury. This process may occur over many years.

- **Dry Face**- The scarred bark never regrows, leaving an area of cracked and withered wood.

- **Epicormic Stem**- A new limb grows out from the scarred area.

- **Overgrowth**- New bark grows over the scar, often leaving a bumpy surface. This new growth strengthens the area around the wound, and it becomes the strongest part of the tree.

As I continued to collect stories from women, I noticed how each story fit into one of these four categories. Some women never recovered from their scars. They had a slow death, cutting themselves away from life, or answered the seductive call of suicide from a pain they could not endure. Others became withered and cracked and descended into bitterness, and they used their wound as their reason for addiction, self-harm, bullying, and wounding others. I met women who were still angry over something that happened sixty years ago, unable or unwilling to move past the toxic events in their past.

Those women made me profoundly sad. Thankfully, they were in the minority.

The vast majority of the women I interviewed fit into the final two categories. They grew from the events that scarred them, finding a new pathway that provided strength and confidence. These were women of resilience. Many had been knocked down numerous times, but each found the strength to continue and became even stronger because of their scar.

I was fascinated by their courage and wondered what made them different from the others. Was it faith, stubbornness, or genetics? Or was it the support of friends, family, and community that enabled them to grow even when their life seemed horrible and the pain unending?

The common thread I found was a powerful commitment to life. That commitment may have stemmed from spiritual faith, a special someone who believed in their worth, or a mysterious inner fire, but all the women found a way to just live, even after tragedy. Like a tree growing out of a rock, there was a seed of life in them which refused to die.

I honor every woman who shared her story with me. While some of the stories are featured in this book, there are many others that are held privately in my heart. As you read these stories, you'll find parallels with your own life. That's because every woman has scars and the accompanying stories about how she got them.

None of us get out of our lives unscathed by pain, disappointment, and loss. Yet, there is something noble and affirming in each of these stories precisely because of the scarring. When you read these stories, you'll realize a few things:

1. You are not alone.

2. You are not broken or unworthy.

3. Your scars make you strong and beautiful.

4. Stories don't always have a happy ending. You may never completely get over what happened to you, but as long as you are alive and trying, you have triumphed over whatever or whoever harmed you.

5. Your story matters, whether you share it publicly or keep it private. The things that scarred you and frightened you contributed to your growth. The wisdom you gained is worth celebrating and sharing as you see fit.

This is not an ordinary book.

This book is different by design. It's not a book you read from cover to cover, although you may if you wish. This book is designed for the busy woman who needs a moment of encouragement.

Place your copy in the kitchen and read a story while the tea brews. Keep it by your bedside table and sneak in a story before bed. Read it on your phone while you are waiting for an appointment or for the kids to finish soccer practice. Because, although each story is placed under a theme, every story in this book stands alone.

I began my professional life as a teacher, and I came from a line of teachers several generations deep. It's in my blood. I can't look at an experience without noticing what I can learn from it. I'm also someone who has sorted her life out on the page since the time she could write.

I still remember the thrill of getting a diary with a real lock and key. When we write about our experiences, we can view them more objectively and begin to make sense of them as we notice themes, patterns, and behaviors that make us who we are. A September 2001 study published in the *Journal of Experimental Psychology* found that when college students wrote about their stressors and challenges, they were able to process and organize them effectively, lessen intrusive thoughts, decrease stress, and improve their cognitive performance.

To that end, I invite you to write in this book! You'll find questions after each story designed to help you consider your own life through the lens of another woman's story. As you write, your self-understanding will expand, and you'll find ways to articulate the things your heart already knows but that your conscious mind may not yet see.

Alternatively, if you are using an e-reader, or don't like writing in books, you can download a free journal that contains all the questions at www.womenofscarclan.com/journal.

However, if you feel unsafe putting your thoughts on paper, I understand your reservations. Long ago, someone who harmed me used my journals against me and I was not able to keep a journal for ten years. When I felt safe enough to journal again, I celebrated and now treasure the time I spend writing every morning. I hope that you can use the questions in a way that supports you, whether you ponder them in your heart or explore them on paper.

You'll also have an opportunity to share your own story if you wish. There is power in sharing your scar with sisters who see your strength and power, even if you cannot see it yet. I believe that when we share who we really are, scars and all, our shame dissipates. When we are heard and seen, we come out of hiding and emerge from behind our fake curtain of having it all together. I hid behind that curtain for a long time, and when I encountered some women who let me tell my story, I was healed in a profound way. Instead of feeling like I was the only one who was screwed up, I learned every woman feels that way about some area of her life. This was liberating!

This is a book of celebration. It is a victory song for women, one we deserve to sing for ourselves and for others.

May you be empowered and encouraged as you read!

"It doesn't interest me what planets are squaring your moon. I want to know if you have touched the center of your own sorrow, if you have been opened by life's betrayals or have become shriveled and closed from fear of further pain. I want to know if you can sit with pain, mine or your own, without moving to hide it or fade it, or fix it."

- Oriah Mountain Dreamer

SECTION 1

Scars Demand Attention

"Lynne, work it harder."

I worked in a hand clinic at one time in my life, providing therapy to people with painful scars from burns, accidents, and surgeries. When a hand is injured, scar tissue can sometimes cause it to contract, limiting movement and usefulness. My job was to help prevent those scars from hardening through exercises, heat, and scar massage.

The first time I had to rub someone's scar, I was worried that I was harming them. My supervisor noted my reluctance and said, "If you don't stretch those scars and encourage patients to move their hands, they may lose all function. *Scars demand attention.*"

Scars do demand our attention, whether they are physical, psychological, or spiritual. We all have them; the mark on our body from an injury, the self-doubt born from a childhood experience, or the panic we feel when we are triggered and brought back to a time when we were terrified and powerless. No woman makes it through life untouched by pain. Whether we hide our scars, wave them as a banner to excuse our behavior, or pretend they don't matter, our scars influence every part of our lives.

In 1992, Dr. Clarissa Pinkola Estes published *Women Who Run with the Wolves* and introduced the concept of Scar Clan, a group of people who experienced a terrible assault of the heart, mind, or body, and survived. She wrote, "For women, tears are the beginning of initiation into Scar Clan, that timeless tribe of women of all colors, all nations, all languages who, down through the ages, have lived through a great something, and yet who stood ground." When I read about Scar Clan for the first time, my heart leapt. I wasn't the only one carrying around pain. It felt good to know that I was part of a tribe of survivors.

Shameful Scars

In my experience, every woman I've ever met is a card-carrying member of the Scar Clan. In movies, myths, and real life, women cannot escape scarring. Most of us are profoundly ashamed of our scars, even though they were done to us and they weren't our fault. Like many of you, I carried a secret scar for many years. I'm afraid to share it, so I will do so right now, partially as a way to massage my own scar and, most importantly, to start our conversation.

During the month of my fourteenth birthday, things began to change for me. I got my first period, realized I looked good to boys, and I was sexually assaulted by the dirty old man next door.

He'd been creeping around me for a long time, always wanting me to sit in his lap, but I was too naive to tell anyone. One day, when I was home alone, bad things happened. When my parents came home, I told my dad. He never said a word to me and then immediately went over to talk to the old man. I don't know what was said, but I never saw that man again.

This was in a rural area in 1976, and things were different. My parents must not have known what else to do, so nothing else was discussed. I had not been raped, there were no visible injuries, and they fixed the problem. Only, the problem wasn't fixed inside me. I started talking to other girls about what happened, including my older cousins. They told me the same thing had happened to them and it was important to stay away from this guy.

I was so angry! How come no one warned me about this horny old man? Why didn't our parents do something to make him stop terrorizing the other young girls in the area?

I was also deeply ashamed. I felt dirty and that I somehow brought this situation on myself. I thought it was my fault.

This situation was a pivotal one for me. I became increasingly afraid of my body, my sexuality, and my beauty. In a few years, I packed on twenty extra pounds that have been with me ever since. I dressed conservatively and didn't date much. I gave up on being pretty and instead aimed to be valued for my intelligence, warmth, and kindness. Being the pretty one was too risky, so I'd be the nice, good one instead, as if they were mutually exclusive.

But all of this was beneath my conscious understanding. I could not figure out why no one wanted to date me. I did have some infatuations and short-lived relationships, but nothing felt right.

This was my introduction to the Scar Clan. It was the first deep wound that left me changed.

My experience was not unique. Almost every young woman has experiences that lead to a fear of men. We have all tasted that terror in the pit of the stomach – the shallow breathing, the desire to run far and fast.

Today, I am grateful for many things about that awful experience. It's taken many years and lots of therapy, but I can see now how brave I was on that day, how cleverly I got away, how hiding my beauty was an understandable reaction, and how much courage it took to live across the road from the man for the rest of my high school years. I'm also thankful that my dad confronted him. My father did not like conflict, yet he stood up for me and I never saw that evil neighbor man again. And today, I'm finally comfortable in my skin and enjoy my sexuality. I've been loved, chosen, and married, more than once. I'm glad to be me; it just took a while to complete the healing journey.

When you are feeling brave, look back at your first scar. Can you see your strength, courage, resilience, and bravery? Regardless of what happened to you and how you reacted to it, *it did not destroy you.* You are here today, reading this book, and having a virtual conversation with me and all your sisters in the Scar Clan. You are more than your scars. You know this, have read it in countless social media memes and self-help books. However, deep inside you, you may not yet believe in your beauty and strength.

That's okay. My prayer is that, by the time you finish this book, you will embrace your value as a beautiful, strong woman who has been through Hell and come back.

The First Scar

Every woman remembers her first serious scar, whether it comes in the early years or during adolescence. These first scars are often the result of someone else's choices. They happen unexpectedly and rob of us our innocence. They teach us to worry and to fear. In the best scenarios, they also teach us to forgive. Sometimes that forgiveness is not possible for a long time, especially in cases of abuse and violation.

Abby was sixteen when we did this interview. She's a very bright young woman from a loving family, and her life looks easy on the outside. She's done well in school, has lots of friends, a job she enjoys, and she excels in sports. Abby has a strong work ethic, an easy laugh, and a magical way with children. She also has a scar that's still healing.

Her older brother was her hero. They were always close until he started drinking, and soon alcohol consumed his life. Everyone tried to talk to him and to get him help, but he wouldn't listen or acknowledge that it was a problem. Abby was so angry about the way he was hurting himself and the family, so they grew distant, even though they were living in the same home.

One night, he was drinking alone in his room and decided to take a drive to see some friends. Abby remembers yelling at him to stay home, to look at his behavior, and to stop hurting their parents. He didn't listen, and it was one of the few times that she didn't tell him that she loved him as he left the house.

Abby saw her parents running out the front door when they got the call about the car accident. Her brother was seriously injured, and he'd broken his neck when his car rolled. The doctors didn't know if he would survive, if he was paralyzed, or if he would fully recover. No one could predict an outcome.

Abby was overcome by grief and sorrow. She felt terrible about her angry words. She was also furious that her beloved brother let alcohol cause so much harm to himself and their family. He was hospitalized in a large city and she couldn't visit him to tell him that she loved him and that she was sorry. It felt like her heart was splitting apart. Abby called her mom and asked her to hold up the phone so she could speak to her brother before his surgery.

It's very painful to see someone you love stalked by demons they can't resist. Abby's brother survived his injuries and is working on his sobriety, but the experience changed Abby. She is more cautious about choosing friends and is stronger in her resolve to avoid the temptations of the teen years. It also made her examine her faith.

"I realized that I had to forgive him, even though I was still angry and sad. I grew up in church and my faith is very important to me. How can I expect to be forgiven if I withhold forgiveness from my own brother? Holding onto my anger was not what God wanted me to do. I had to forgive my brother and, when I did, we both felt better."

Your first scar could still be haunting you or you may have healed it long ago. Consider re-framing it as your initiation, as a rite of passage into womanhood. Look back at that event and notice your courage. You found a way to survive, and despite the pain, terror, and trauma of your first scar, you're still here. You developed what is called tensile strength, the ability to withstand more pressure because of the strength that first wound inflicted upon you. Like Abby, you may have had to dig deep to forgive the person who harmed you, not because you condone their actions, but to free yourself from the pain of unforgiveness. I am proud of you for moving past your first scar. Congratulations!

Looking in the Mirror

Explore these questions in your journal, write the answers in this book, or contemplate them while you go for a walk.

- When you received your first wound, were you made of hard or soft wood? What are you made of today?

- What strengths did you develop from your first wound?

"You gain strength, courage, and confidence by every experience in which you really stop to look fear in the face. You are able to say to yourself, 'I lived through this horror. I can take the next thing that comes along.'"

- Eleanor Roosevelt

SECTION 2

Courage

"The best protection any woman can have … is courage."

– Elizabeth Cady Stanton

Marina Elena is exhausted.

She and her husband, Jorge, just walked from Venezuela to Ecuador with their toddler, Gabriella. The journey took three months and was filled with danger. The family had no money, so they slept outdoors or in bus terminals. They ate bread and drank water. When they crossed the border into Colombia, men offered them $5000 dollars for Gabriella, saying that she would die anyway so her parents may as well give her the chance to live and get some money for their new life. Later in the journey, the family encountered bodies of dead children by the side of the road; victims of cold, illness or malnutrition.

I met the young family at a restaurant in Cuenca, Ecuador where they were hoping to get help from a local charity. I gave them a menu and told them to order whatever they wished. They were overwhelmed and ordered one bowl of soup to share and a glass of water. Maria Elena's eyes filled with tears as she told me that they had to leave their infant son behind with relatives in Venezuela, fearing that he was too young to endure the trip. They hoped to find work and earn enough money to bring their son and other family members out of Venezuela in the future. But tonight, they just wanted a safe place to sleep.

There comes a point in every woman's life when she must have the courage to look at her situation with honesty. Facing the truth is difficult. It feels easier to pretend that everything is okay, that the person harming you will change, or that other women have a harder life than you do. But the women of Scar Clan begin their journey by looking and facing the reality of their situation, and you can find your courage by listening to the stories of other women.

Speaking the Truth

When I first started this project, I put a request out on Facebook for women with stories of courage to come forward and share them with me. The first interview I did was with a woman I'd met at a marketing seminar years before, someone I'd·liked instantly. She told me a story that still amazes me years later, and I pray I will do it, and her, justice as I share it with you.

Amethyst Wyldfyre was the name she chose years ago. I don't know the reason but am confident it was carefully selected to honor a milestone on her personal and spiritual journey. When we spoke, she'd just legally changed her name to Emerald Peaceful GreenForest.

Picture a tall, slender woman whose soul shines from her eyes when she smiles. She is a creative entrepreneur and successful public speaker, and Emerald has reinvented herself before. A native New Englander, Emerald has walked a spiritual path for many years through prayer, meditation, yoga, ceremony, and study.

Like many of us, Emerald gained her first scars in childhood. Her father was an alcoholic. Both of her parents abused her. Her first boyfriend was addicted to drugs. She overcame many challenges to build a good life for herself.

Emerald had an adult son living with her with a serious drug problem that spilled over several years. She shared, "He'd used every possible drug you can imagine. Heroin. Cocaine. Spice. LSD. He tried everything you can imagine, including multiple suicide attempts."

When Emerald discovered him passed out in the basement, she noticed his laptop nearby. He'd been using bitcoin to buy more heroin and fentanyl. When he awoke, he was furious, and when she tried to intervene, he attacked her, said he was going to kill her, and told her she had to stay off her phone and remain in the basement. He went upstairs and locked the door, trapping her inside.

Emerald thought this would be the end of her life. However, instead of panicking, she started to pray and meditate. She called on Jesus, angels, and all the spiritual beings who were important to her. After some time passed, she heard a voice telling her to go and unbolt the outside basement door – one of those big, old-fashioned doors that angled down a short stairway from the ground down into the basement. She obeyed, and as she was unbolting, she heard something heavy dragging across the outer door.

Her son came back downstairs screaming. Emerald says, "I tried a couple more times to ask him if I could go and use the bathroom. He said, 'No you're not fucking going anywhere. I'm calling somebody to come and take you to the river and cut you up in little pieces.' " Emerald continued to pray and meditate, trying to stay as calm as she could. Finally, her son went upstairs, and she heard a voice telling her to go *now*. She shoved open the blocked outer door and ran down the street into the woods. She clung to a tree in the forest trembling.

When Emerald called 911, the man who arrived was Officer Friend, and soon he got her out of the woods and into safety. Even his name felt like a blessing. She added, "There are incredible spiritual tools and an unbelievable potent web of support around us all the time. The thing that allowed me to move through the eye of the needle was deeply acknowledging and surrendering to what I like to call the "invisible realm of support". It was all around me in that basement and in the forest. It's always there for each of us."

The story was not over at all. Emerald had to tell her story to three policemen, first Officer Friend, then his supervisor, and finally a detective. Each time, she wondered if she should edit it to protect her son, especially when she learned that he was going to be charged with felony kidnapping and assault.

Each time she told the story, her throat started to tighten and clench. "Women are taught to stay silent, to protect our abusers and to protect our children, no matter the cost. If I told the truth of this situation, my son would be charged with a felony that would haunt him for the rest of his life." After meeting with the supervisor, Emerald was conflicted. She asked the Sergeant for a little time to think it over. Then he told her, "You have a choice here. You can stop now or talk to the detective about what happened. Whatever you decide, that will be your life from now on."

Those words gave Emerald the strength she needed to tell the truth. She knew it was time to break the cycle of abuse and choose her life. She owed it to herself and to her son to bring his behavior out into the open so that he could get some help, or at least be in an environment where he would be away from drugs. She told her story to the detective and her son was arrested and charged.

Two days after the event, Emerald heard a voice that told her she was no longer Amethyst Wyldfyre. That part of her died in the basement. Now she was Emerald Peaceful GreenForest. She accepted this message and began to purge her old identity, finding the peace and healing her new name carried. She burned sage in the basement, wrote in her journal each day, prayed, and performed spiritual ceremonies to release the pain of her experiences in order to embrace her new life.

It was difficult to ask for help. Like many of us, Emerald feels more comfortable being the helper instead of the recipient of help. It was not comfortable, because she didn't want to vilify her son or become the object of pity. She told me, "When in a traumatic experience, the last thing you want to do is invite energies that will perpetuate and make heroic the trauma. What's heroic is not the trauma. We actually don't want to keep creating trauma in order to feel or acknowledge ourselves as heroic. I dearly would like to see a world where we dispense with the idea of having to be in trauma in order to recognize that we're heroic and courageous.

"We have a culture that glorifies trauma. Social media can make us addicted to creating another trauma so that we can get applause from the audience. I didn't want that. So, I made a very specific request for prayer on Facebook. I had very clear boundaries about what I wanted. I said that I didn't want people to see me as a victim even though the court system was labelling me in this way. I don't blame my son. What I did want were prayers for positive energy for the good of the all. Period. I closed my request with, 'Do not tell me you're sorry. If you do, I will delete you as a friend.' "

Friends complied with her request and sent her love and light. It took a long time for Emerald to heal from this experience and become a new person, one who embraced life and peace and refused to give any more of her energy to trauma. She remembered a story she'd heard about a t-shirt company in Boston called "Life is Good".

After the attacks at the Boston Marathon, this company created a shirt with the motto, "Nothing is Stronger than Love". This shirt raised thousands of dollars for people harmed in that event. This motto stuck in Emerald's mind and became her new mantra.

It was difficult to sit through the court proceedings, to testify, and see her son convicted. Yet, each time she was feeling the old pull of trauma, Emerald repeated, "Nothing is Stronger than Love" in her mind until she felt calm and centered.

Today, Emerald focuses her energy, prayers, and mind on thriving instead of trauma. It's a practice and one that requires attention and intention. She will never forget those terrifying moments in the basement nor the peace she found in the forest that day. Bit by bit, she has reclaimed her life and learned to live in the power and energy of her new name, Emerald Peaceful GreenForest.

Emerald's story resonated with me deeply because I am a mother too. Like many mothers, there are times when I had to decide if I was going to smooth something over for my children or let them face the consequence of their actions. Women are taught that family comes first, that it is important to protect a family member's reputation and community standing. Almost every woman I interviewed for this project spoke of the struggle to speak the truth about someone who harmed them, especially when that person was a family member.

Many have also had to choose whether to use our scar to garner attention or sympathy. When you've kept a secret for so long, there is an intoxicating freedom in telling the truth. I remember when I first left an abusive marriage, I told almost everyone about it. I needed positive feedback and support because I was terrified. Over time, I realized that I didn't want that story to define me, and as I healed, I stopped seeing myself as a victim and I no longer used that story as my introduction.

Many women bond by sharing their scars. This sharing can be a way to demonstrate solidarity, celebrate strength, and exchange intimate stories with other women. However, Emerald's story reminds us to pay attention to our motives to ensure we are not waving the victim flag in an unhealthy way. Her ideas about the addiction of sharing pain are worth considering closely.

Looking in the Mirror

- Have you ever struggled over deciding to speak about your scar in order to protect the one who wounded you?

- When you share the story of your wounding with others, do you feel lighter or slightly icky afterwards?

"Remembering what you've been through and how that has strengthened your mindset can lift you out of a negative brain loop and help you bypass those weak, one-second impulses to give in. Even if you're feeling low and beat down by life right now, I guarantee you can think of a time or two when you overcame odds and tasted success."

- David Gogginst

It's Not Fair

When you are faced with a scarring situation, it can be very helpful to know that other women have faced pain, trauma and painful situations and endured. Even so, some women's stories feel like something from a movie.

Yoshi Mizono is amazed that she is still alive. At 96, her eyes are bright, and her smile is warm, even if it is hard to walk. I met Yoshi in Cuenca, Ecuador, where she lives in an apartment in the same building as her daughter, Lynn. Over a wonderful Japanese meal, Yoshi told me her story.

Yoshi's parents emigrated to the United States from Japan in the early 1900's. The family settled in San Francisco with very little money but with a strong desire to make a better life for their family. Many members of the family farmed vegetables to sell on rented farmland in Half Moon Bay. When Yoshi was four years old, her mother became very ill with cancer and eventually passed away at the age of 45. Yoshi noticed how the nurses helping her mother seemed powerful and confident, like they knew what to do in every situation. She decided she wanted to become a nurse when she grew up, although it seemed impossible. Her family had no money for tuition.

After the attack on Pearl Harbor in 1941, all people of Japanese descent were ordered into camps. Yoshi, her father, and her brothers and sisters read the newspapers and learned about the order. They were afraid and ended up burning all of their Japanese possessions in fear that it could be used as evidence against them. They packed suitcases with bare necessities and boarded a hired bus to San Mateo, California, and from there caught a train to Topaz, Utah, unsure of what awaited them there. The vast majority went quietly and willingly into the camps, thus earning them the title, "The Quiet Americans". Her eldest brother was sent to a higher security camp, Tulelake in California, as he was one of a small minority that questioned the imprisonment of American citizens. Yoshi decided to stay quiet.

Life in the desert camp felt strange. They lived in hastily built sheds with little privacy. The walls were thin and not airtight. Yoshi remembers being covered with a layer of dust when she woke in the mornings. It was a frightening time filled with much uncertainty and worry. They were prisoners and their country of origin was in a bitter war with their new homeland.

The people in the camp made the best of their lives during this time, forming a community, taking on jobs, and organizing events that complied with the many rules. In time, there was school, hospital, worship services, and even a band. Yoshi worked as an aide in the camp hospital, which she enjoyed immensely. She made a very good friend, Elaine, and enjoyed learning patient care skills.

By 1945, the war with Japan was ending. People could leave the camp if they had a job. However, Yoshi and her family could not return to their vegetable farm in Half Moon Bay, as those rental agreements and their possessions were lost while they were interred. But then a miracle happened. Yoshi was given the opportunity by the government to go to nursing school on the East Coast. Her dream of becoming a nurse was manifesting.

Yoshi and Elaine traveled to Pennsylvania to attend nursing school at Pennsylvania Hospital, the oldest hospital in the United States. They read an advertisement for domestic workers and secured work in the same household, which provided them room and board. Yoshi was the cook. She did not really know how to cook American style food, but she figured it out, and her employer especially loved her chocolate cake. When she graduated from nursing school, Yoshi returned to California and began her nursing career. Eventually, she married George, her brother's friend who was interred at the same camp she was in Utah. George and Yoshi were happily married for 48 years.

I asked Yoshi if she was angry about being imprisoned in the camp. She said it was hard, but people there wanted to prove their loyalty to the United States, so they did their best to obey all the rules and be peaceful. Yoshi and her family relied on their Christian faith for comfort. It was a difficult experience, but her family was together, and they worked hard to endure the adversity, trusting in God to protect them. They had very little before they were imprisoned in the camp, and even less when they left, but they had each other as well as a strong desire to build a new life. Her father was a wonderful gardener and found ways to support the family when they left the camps.

It seemed strange to me that Yoshi was at peace with the events of her past. As a young woman, she was imprisoned for her race, not for anything she did. She lived in harsh conditions behind barbwire fences in the middle of a desert in a country she called home. But she told me that anger and bitterness were not healthy emotions. She learned to focus on the future and to see how God used all these events to help her achieve her dream of being a nurse.

After a long career in nursing, raising her two children, and the death of her husband, Yoshi thought she'd die soon and moved into a retirement center. She lived there many years but later decided to accompany her daughter to Ecuador when she was 89 years old, ready for another radical change and a new adventure.

When I first heard Yoshi's story, I was angry. It seemed so unfair that her family lost their freedom for something that they didn't do. As I write this in 2019, people all over the globe are grappling with the impact of political decisions on their personal lives. There are no easy answers to immigration, conflict between nations, or gun control, and it feels as if there is a war going on against women, children and even Mother Earth herself. It is almost impossible to watch the news or look at social media without despair. Many feel hopeless to effect change, as if we are imprisoned too.

Yet, Yoshi taught me something important. She had a choice in the internment camp. She could have become angry and bitter; it was her right. Yet, she believed those emotions would harm her. She focused instead on what she could do to improve her future, trusting that God would protect her. Yoshi never gave up on her dream or her faith, and she acted with courage and conviction even when she was afraid.

Looking in the Mirror

- What do you do when things feel unfair?

- Do you believe that even painful events can bring you to a better future?

Our hearts carry the facts, but it is how we experienced those facts, and what we did with them, that will reveal who we really are.

- Gunilla Norris

The Power of Faith

This is a book about faith, in the Divine and in your own strength. The women in this book have a wide variety of beliefs and spiritual practices. While you may not agree with how all the women in this book practice their faith, I pray that, as you read, you are inspired to deepen your faith in your own way.

Robin grew up in a home full of secrets. All the women were sexually abused by a family member, which led to addictions and deep pain. The family had wealth and looked enviable from the outside, but daily life was horrific. Robin doesn't remember anyone ever telling her that she was loved or lovable. She was told that her father left when she was born and wanted nothing to do with her.

One day, when she was thirteen, she walked by the ringing telephone and picked it up. The man on the line was her father. He was a good man who lived in a double-wide trailer, and Robin moved in with him when she was fourteen. She dropped out of high school and began a life of partying.

Later, she started dating a bartender who could get her drinks even though she was underage. When she met his mother, Margaret, Robin was astounded. This woman looked at her like she mattered. She'd tell Robin how her smile lit up the room, and she never said anything when Robin spent the night with her son. "Margaret never said anything judgmental to me. I'd never met anyone like her. She just loved and accepted me." Then, one day, Margaret asked Robin if she could pray for her and lead her toward faith in Christ.

Robin became what she calls a radical Christian, devoting her life to evangelism and ministry. Again, her life looked good on the outside, but still she carried deep pain from the trauma and abuse she experienced as a child. She married twice, a man with addictions who could not stay clean, and then to man who cheated on her. She started to drink a bit in secret to cope. When her father died, Robin was devastated. When she was cleaning out his house, she found a huge jar of painkillers, more than 500 tablets, and this would be her undoing.

Robin spent the next ten years in active addiction to painkillers and alcohol. She owned a business and seemed functional but would have five-day binges that left her in bed, unable to even get up and use the bathroom. Her bedroom was full of bottles, and every time she'd wake, she'd just drink more. When Robin Williams committed suicide, Robin started to think she should kill herself. The thought was very seductive, because she felt powerless and separated from God. She had a gun and imagined herself pulling the trigger and ending her misery.

Something snapped inside of Robin, and she started scrolling through her phone, randomly dialing numbers until someone answered. Rhonda, a friend who she had not seen in a long time, picked up the phone and came over. She got Robin in the shower and immediately called her pastor.

Robin went to a Christian rehab center where she finally addressed all the scars from her past and began to heal. During therapy there, she was able to talk about the abuse in her childhood and come to a place of forgiveness. She forgave the family member who committed the sexual abuse, her mother for not protecting her, and then finally forgave herself.

"In the old days, if you killed someone, their dead body was draped over yours and you had to walk around with that rotting flesh on your back. When I could not forgive, I carried all the poison on my back. In the Bible, the word forgiveness means "to throw off". When I was able to throw off my past and forgive, my life changed."

Today, Robin is happy and healthy. She is active in ministry and is working toward founding a house where women in addiction treatment can stay and reclaim their lives. She's often invited to speak to church groups and share the story of her new life in Christ.

"Addiction is a sign of a spiritual malady. We all have a longing for a relationship with the Divine, whether we find that connection in a church, synagogue, mosque, or meditation group. I tried to fill up the holes in my soul with drugs and alcohol and almost lost my life because I forgot who I was: a child of God who is worthy of love."

Robin has maintained her sobriety for many years, repaired her relationships with her children, friends, and family members, and is an active advocate for those who suffer.

"I don't believe you have to belong to any specific religion or follow strict rules. That's bondage and Christ came to set us free. Instead, if you want to know God, if you are seeking God, you will be found. God is not hiding from you. By myself, I am nothing. But because I've been saved by love, more than once, I am willing to do all I can to point other people towards the love of God."

The women of Scar Clan often rely on faith to sustain them. Robin believes that her faith saved her life, and I heard the same story repeated by many of the women interviewed in this book. Perhaps the experience of a deep wound removes some of our defenses so that Divine Love can enter? That Love may show up in the eyes of a kind stranger, a miraculous event, or in a spiritual book. When we are experiencing deep despair, we can find great comfort in faith communities, spiritual music, rituals, and the belief that there is something larger than ourselves. My faith has sustained me through every day of my life and for that I am profoundly grateful.

And yet, I know women who have been harmed by spiritual leaders. Abuse by clergy, retreat leaders, or trusted teachers can leave deep marks on our soul. In those situations, it can be difficult to separate the behavior of human beings from the spiritual teachings they represent.

If you have been harmed by a religious or spiritual teacher, be very gentle with yourself. You may feel inspired to explore other forms of religious or spiritual practice that don't trigger painful memories. You may find a walk in the woods or a silent meditation practice is the best way to connect with your soul. The road you take to faith doesn't matter as much as a willingness to accept that you are, and always have been, loved by the Creator. When you are ready to connect with Divine Love, that love will be waiting for you with open arms.

Looking in the Mirror

- When did you experience help that arrived from an unexpected source?

- Have you had any experiences which felt miraculous to you?

The Silenced Singer

Through a series of rather miraculous events, I was invited to a birthday party while I was in the final stages of editing this book. While I was at the party, I witnessed a stunning act of bravery – a woman getting up to sing for her family and friends.

Aurora was born with an incredible voice. She loved to sing and started to perform publicly at age fourteen. She could sing anything, but she was most drawn to classical singing, so she pursued that training all through her high school and university days. Aurora loved to bring joy to others with her voice. Music was her profession as well as her avocation. When she sang, she felt transported.

Aurora was also gifted with a tremendous sense of humor. She became a professional clown, so when she wasn't singing or acting in musical theatre, she was clowning around, literally. Her life wasn't easy or perfect, but she was living in her passions and she was very happy.

When Aurora discovered a lump in her throat, she sensed that something was dangerously wrong. She decided to have the most invasive surgical treatment, even though it would cost her the ability to sing. The lump ended up being cancerous, so her decision was very wise. However, her surgery left lasting scars.

Aurora had to learn how to speak again. Her new voice sounded strange to her – it was deep, raspy, and rough. While she could produce sounds, she no longer had the ability to modulate or sing in tune. It was disconcerting. She grieved her lost days singing on stages and performing in musicals.

To further complicate matters, Aurora has bipolar disorder, which means that her emotions can swing rapidly and unpredictably. She's had it since childhood but wasn't diagnosed or formally treated until adulthood. Singing and performing helped Aurora maintain emotional stability and joy. Now, those avenues were closed to her.

Aurora is a woman of deep faith. She depends on her spirituality and the rituals of her faith practice. After her experience with cancer, her faith helped her maintain her emotions and find new creative outlets, including art.

At the birthday party, Aurora's friends arranged for music and dancing with a local singer. The room was full of family and friends who all inhaled sharply when the entertainer asked her to join him. He didn't know about her lost voice.

"Total Eclipse of the Heart" by Bonnie Tyler was cued up on the karaoke machine. Aurora went up to the front of the room and sang. Her voice didn't sound like it used to, but no one cared. Her laughter and joyful smile lit up the room.

I was able to talk with Aurora after the party and discuss what that moment meant to her. She told me that she never believed she'd sing again because she just couldn't make anything beautiful come from her throat. She'd found a way to make peace with the loss of her singing and got accustomed to the sound of her new speaking voice. It took eight years, but she was healed from the trauma of her cancer, both physically and emotionally. But on the night of the party, she realized she had a choice. She could stay quiet or she could get up and sing a favorite song, even if it wasn't going to be in tune. And Aurora did sing, loudly and joyfully.

This powerful moment touched me deeply. Like many, I don't like to fail. I'd rather stick with things I know I can do well than try something out of my comfort zone and risk public failure or humiliation. The biggest gift I've received from my scars is the ability to stop worrying about what other people think and take those risks to achieve something I want.

There comes a moment in life when you must decide if fear is going to keep you small. The women of Scar Clan have already looked fear in the eye. By virtue of surviving and overcoming pain in our past, we've toughened up a bit. We are more comfortable with uncertainty and the potential for embarrassment. We've already conquered something that might have destroyed us. We've become like Aurora, able to sing for our own joy, regardless of what anyone else might think.

That's freedom.

Looking in the Mirror

- How have you become braver over time?

- What do you do when you are wondering what someone else will think of your actions?

"You have to take risks. We will only understand the miracle of life fully when we allow the unexpected to happen."

- Paulo Coelho

Giving Up to Become

Martha Strom is a poet. Marty to her friends, she's had a remarkable and unusual journey, one that required great courage. Marty became a member of the Scar Clan in a period of stunning success, when it appeared that everything in her life was perfect.

Marty was a rising star in academia. She graduated with honors from Boston University with a degree in English. Soon after, Marty obtained her PhD from Princeton and became well known for her articles on literary criticism. She taught at Princeton, Brandeis, and then in the Harvard Business School.

In 1985, Marty was enjoying her work at Harvard. During this time, she was introduced to the Seth books, the channeled works of Jane Roberts, and became deeply interested in spirituality and mysticism. She began to work with various tools to connect with her spiritual guides and began to receive repeated messages that she was to become a poet. Soon, Marty was not able to leave her apartment.

She jokes, "When I went crazy, it was in a literary way. I'd studied writers who had mental breakdowns and didn't even realize that I was having one myself." In the eyes of the world, Marty was falling apart. But in her mind, she was becoming a poet.

After some time, Marty lost her job at Harvard, and eventually had to fly to Atlanta where her parents lived. Her family gave her the much-needed support, but her condition continued to worsen, and she was admitted to a state mental health facility. "My family was terribly worried about me. I'd given up Harvard, my career, my home, all my financial resources, and, it appeared, my sanity. However, I knew that I was okay, and that belief gave me the strength and courage to go on."

Slowly, Marty recovered some of her health. She was able to leave the institution because her counselor believed in her. She started to write poetry. She lived with her parents for a time and then with other family members, eventually moving to New York and getting a few jobs in publishing, all the while supported by outpatient therapy and medication. She wrote more poetry and felt she was beginning to think and view the world as a poet. But Marty did not have an ordinary life. Her mental illness caused continual challenges, some quite dangerous and heartbreaking.

Marty believes that her life has been about giving things up so that she could focus on what was most important to her. She gave up her academic career and let go of many things the world deems important. Yet, she gained the freedom to be herself and live a life that suited her. Her writing and her spirituality sustain her, as well as the love of her family and friends.

"I was raised to be a housewife with a man who supports me. That life was not for me. Then, I tried to become a professor, celebrated for my intelligence. That did not work for me either. Instead, I learned to listen to my higher power and follow the guidance I was given.

Even during the darkest times, my life had meaning, and that made all the difference. I have a mental illness that requires medication and treatment, but along with it I've found the courage to be myself, to make poems and art, and to live. My story is a story of coming into my real identity. My path was difficult, but I am still here and able to write. I have become a poet and I am grateful."

Marty's story inspired me because she has a life-long illness which will, most likely, never be cured and only managed. Like many members of the Scar Clan, she did not expect her life to unfold as it did. Her situation might be viewed as pitiful by some in that she lost her grand career, hopes for financial success, and at times, control of her life. Yet, Marty inspires me because she's found ways to experience joy, creativity, and satisfaction, despite an illness that can be unpredictable and frightening. Rather than focusing on what she's lost, she focuses on celebrating what she has. What courage and resilience!

Looking in the Mirror

- Have you had to give things up for your dreams?

- When you consider the most challenging periods in your life, what moments of courage can you celebrate and be proud of?

"What would life be if we had no courage to attempt anything?"

- Vincent van Gogh

It Runs in the Family

Angela Barnes, the oldest child, grew up in a unique family. Both her parents used wheelchairs and coped with severe physical challenges. Angela wrote two books about her mother's remarkable story. These are Angela's words, used with her permission:

"Janet Barnes was the longest living quadriplegic recorded in the Guinness World Records. Born on October 9, 1928, she was also the oldest living quadriplegic at the time of her death, September 13, 2013 (83 years, 5 months and 12 days). She was a living miracle. Her story will challenge, encourage and inspire, as well prove to you that miracles really do happen."

Every day, Janet Barnes did what most of us would consider impossible. She excelled in school, went to a vocational school to learn photo retouching and was an early pioneer of "working from home". She married her beloved Harold, someone who accepted her as she was and whom she also accepted as he was (a paraplegic). They both had a real zest for living and accomplished more than many able-bodied people.

They had four children. They managed a household. They worked together and invented or adapted equipment so that they could function independently. They were entrepreneurs, they worked many jobs, they bought and renovated houses to accommodate their physical challenges, and they provided sufficiently for their family.

After more than 35 years of marriage, Harold died, but Janet remained strong and continued to learn. She became proficient in computer programming and continued to work from home. Later, she volunteered as a foster grandmother and teacher's assistant. Her quick wit and loving demeanor helped children open themselves up to their potential. She was affectionately known as "Grandma Janet" by thousands of children, parents and people in the community.

Janet Barnes appreciated the beauty all around her, captured in her artwork through painting, crocheting and writing, and her legacy continues to challenge and encourage and inspire us to be all that we can be – to prove that miracles really do happen!

I was fortunate to meet Angela while she was writing the books about her mother's remarkable life. Angela inherited strength, courage, and determination from her parents, along with a deep well of creativity. Her personal story is full of faith and courage as well. Angela knows that nothing is impossible, that pain and challenge are part of every life, and that self-pity should be avoided at all costs. There are many layers to both Janet and Angela Barnes' stories, with enough inspirational material to fill several books.

Janet and Harold came from extremely challenging childhoods. Harold grew up in an orphanage and Janet grew up with a family who neglected her terribly. They easily could have been bitter and sour people, but instead chose to be positive and live life as independently as possible. The family motto was, "There is nothing we can't do, it just might take us a little longer."

Janet loved to research and had an eclectic faith, which embraced practices from many traditions. Above all, she had a relationship with God, whom she talked with regularly. She faced incredible challenges in her life, including constant illnesses, dreadful injuries after being struck by a car, and medical procedures and mistakes that caused lasting damage to her frail body. Her faith helped her endure a life that few of us can imagine, and she somehow maintained a positive outlook. Janet also experienced miracles and always had faith that things would be okay. She refused to quit and give up on life. She taught that courage to Angela, who relied on it during the ups and downs in her own remarkable life.

When I asked Angela what she learned about courage from her parents, she replied, "My parents set a very high bar for me. From them I learned that courage is not just one action. It's a daily commitment to do the things you need to do whether you feel like it or not. Courage is always moving forward, even if the outcome of your efforts isn't exactly what you want or expect. My parents taught me how to make the best of every situation, how to keep my eyes open to life, seeing both the good and the bad, and how to decide to not let anything stand in your way."

There is much you can learn from Angela and her parents. When I read her books, I lost my ability to feel sorry for myself or my situation. If they could create a productive and positive life with the challenges in front of them, I knew I could too. Janet and Angela faced life with a focus on celebrating what was possible instead of what they could not do, and this is a trait you'll see repeated in the Scar Clan.

We all face heartbreaking loss at some point in our lives. Some of us face heartbreak more than once. Our scars can make us bitter or better; it is our choice! Janet and Angela chose courageously and discovered that anything is possible, even it takes a long time.

For more information about this inspirational family, visit 90poundheavyweight.org. For Angela's writing go to heartspokenwords. com.

Looking in the Mirror

- How does Janet's story inspire you?

- When you experience self-pity, what do you do to lift yourself from it?

"Never bend your head. Always hold it high. Look the world straight in the eye."

- Helen Keller

The Dark Side of Strength

Tina Forsyth is a smart, practical, and successful entrepreneur. She is famous in her circles for being a problem solver, strategist, and someone who can get things done. I've been lucky enough to know her for a long time and I helped Tina publish her two outstanding books for women entrepreneurs. I could tell you a lot about her professional accomplishments, which are many, but there is a private side to Tina that is equally impressive, not because of what she accomplished, but because of what she learned and how those lessons have impacted her business.

Like many of us, Tina excelled in the professional world and got her scars at home. She was married to a man named Dan and had two wonderful little girls. Everything looked fine from the outside, but their marriage wasn't working, and it never really had. After many years and efforts to make things work, Tina asked for a divorce.

Suddenly, Dan became Dani. Over time, he told Tina that he was transgendered and wanted to become a woman. Finally, things made sense! She'd always blamed herself for their lackluster romantic life, but now Dan's constant unhappiness and complaining added up.

"His decision to become a female was not as painful as I thought it might have been. I believe people should be free to be and live however they wish. However, it was hard to cope with the reactions of some of our friends and family members."

It was hard to be a single parent and an entrepreneur with a team of employees and multiple projects. She was surprised by the emotional toll of being the sole provider for her children. It felt like the weight of the world was on her shoulders. She also realized that, like many strong women, she was the one who everyone depended on, and this made her feel like a martyr, having to put on a happy face even when she was sad. She could never ask for help, because she was the helper in her family, friendships, and her business.

Suddenly, Tina's passion for her business started to fade. Clients and staff members left, revenues were down, and the face of internet business started to change. She realized that she could no longer pretend that everything was great and that she had it all under control. It was time to stop trying to be all things to all people and trying to solve every problem that came her way.

She started talking to other entrepreneurs and discovered they were experiencing the same downturn. It was a relief to talk openly about what was happening with people who understood, and Tina soon came to realize that working harder would not fix these problems. She needed to take some time to decide what she really wanted. She needed to learn how to ask for help.

Tina worked hard to understand her patterns. She realized that she loved being independent, taking care of other people, and taking on every challenge because, deep down, she was taking care of other people in hopes that they would take care of her. When that did not happen, she just worked harder and tried to hide her resentment.

"I learned that many professional women are like me. We say, 'I am woman, hear me roar.' We get stuff done and make things happen. The dark side of that strength is exhaustion, burnout, and a deep sadness that we hide from everyone, even ourselves. I just craved support but didn't believe I could ask for it."

It's been a journey over several years. Tina's rebuilt her business and is learning to trust her intuition and spirituality instead of only relying on her mind and efforts to solve problems. She's learned how to ask for help and receive support. She's also free of the need to pretend that everything is perfect and she has it all together.

Interestingly, Tina's clients struggle with the same issues; the light and dark side of being a powerful woman. The online industry is full of people who carefully curate their images to show a perfect life that appears easy and blissful. When Tina was brave enough to talk about her struggles for support and balance, other women with similar scars stepped forward and some hired her. It was not easy to share her scars and admit that life and business were not perfect, but telling the truth, looking at her patterns, and asking for help made a tremendous difference in her life and her business.

Tina now believes that many professional women go through stages in their careers. First, they try to prove themselves and their stamina, working harder and harder and taking on any challenge that comes their way. That drive and independence is useful and can create great results. However, it is not sustainable and leads to exhaustion, physically and emotionally.

That period of exhaustion brings an opportunity, a chance to look at your relationships, work, health, and every part of your life, and then decide if you are happy. Tina was not happy and gave herself permission to let go of her marriage and seemingly indefatigable spirit. She learned to show her scars, find a balance between giving and receiving, and realized that she was not alone in these challenges. Tina's found a way to work and live from a middle ground of trust; trust in herself and her intuition, trust that she is worthy of giving and receiving support, and trust that she can be both successful and tell the truth.

Looking in the Mirror

- Have you tried to pretend that you have it all together even when you were struggling?

- How have you learned to ask for support?

"When I dare to be powerful - to use my strength in the service of my vision, then it becomes less and less important whether I am afraid."

- Audre Lorde

Hiding Behind a Smile

While I was researching this book, it felt like each interview was holy; the conversations sacred. There was laughter and tears, and I felt honored to be hearing these personal and profound stories. I relished each one.

Then, when it was time to write the book and find a way to weave them all together, I floundered. I procrastinated, took other work projects, and wasted time scrolling through Facebook. This behavior mystified me.

I am a full-time professional writer and teach writing to others. When I ghostwrite books for clients, write courses for my students, or write in my journal, I love it and can happily work for hours. I was embarrassed to admit that this writing coach was sabotaging a project near and dear to her heart.

So, I followed the advice I gave my writing students. I made a commitment to launching the book on a specific day. I cleared my calendar for six months and didn't take on new clients or launch new classes. I pre-paid for some of the publishing services so that I would not back out— I hate to lose money! I even told friends and my entire email list what I was doing so that I created peer pressure for myself. I used my spiritual tools as well. I wrote a vision statement for myself and my readers. I created intentions and prayers, did meditations, and worked with healers and counselors. I used every tool and technique I knew of and took writing classes to learn new ones.

Still, the progress was slow. I became more disciplined and set daily writing goals and created periods where I didn't leave home except to walk my dogs to force me to stay home and write. On these writing retreats, I would have a breakthrough one day and a breakdown the next. I could not figure out why I was going so slowly.

So, as my normal practice, I prayed and asked for help, then starting writing in my journal. All of my life, I have tried to deny, cover up, distract, and heal from my pain as quickly as possible. Like everyone, I've had my fair share of sorrow. It is much more comfortable for me to talk about happy things.

I can still hear Grandma Grace telling me that it was important to smile and find things to be glad about, even when you were having a hard day. Grandma knew about hard days. She had lots of them, but always seemed to find something good to focus on.

Grace Stahlhut was a frail person physically but a giantess of faith and spirit. She was plagued with poor health most of her life. She had five children, but each were spaced five years apart, not because she planned it that way, but because she'd lost so many babies in between.

She never let illness define her or stop her from living a busy and productive life. She'd been invited to attend Art School in Chicago in the 1920's but did not have the funds for tuition, so she became a teacher instead. She married my grandfather, Herman, right before the Great Depression, and they worked hard to survive on a farm in Iowa with very little money but lots of love.

Years later, when I came along, Grandma and Grandpa lived in a town where Grandpa worked as a mechanic for the local John Deere tractor dealer. Grandma spent her time creating. She could sew beautifully, draw and paint, taught herself taxidermy, wrote poems and stories, and cooked mouthwatering foods. She had a particular interest in dolls. She made stuffed animals and dolls with china heads, hands, and feet. People brought her old dolls which she repaired and dressed. The newspaper even did a big story on Grandma Grace calling her the "Doll Lady of Iowa". When she died, she had so many collectible dolls in her house that it took a full day to auction them all off.

My grandmother had many superpowers, but one of the most curious was that she loved her family unconditionally. She simply would not hear a bad word about anyone in her family. She thought we were all wonderful and told us so frequently. I remember my older cousin sneaking outside for a cigarette during a family gathering and someone snitching to Grandma. I can still hear her saying, "Oh no, he would never smoke." She was a brilliant woman and certainly knew exactly what was going on, but she refused to admit that one of her precious grandchildren could do anything wrong. She was a stubbornly positive person who made it her mission to see the best in life and in her family.

I never understood her refusal to believe anything but the best of us – her tribe of imperfect children, grandchildren, and great grandchildren – until I had a miscarriage. She knew the value of human life because she'd had so many lives slip through her fingers. When a child entered the world, healthy and thriving, she knew it was to be loved and nurtured.

Grace Stahlhut was a force of nature, but one of the most loving, kind, and creative people on the planet. She was also quietly stubborn, like velvet covering steel. Grandma was never one to dwell in sadness. When things got tough, she got busy creating, even when she was weak and hurting.

Today I see that Grandma was the first member of the Scar Clan I knew. She left a deep mark on me. She taught me the value of faith, family, and creating beauty just to make the world brighter. She was so curious and loved to learn, and she could figure out how to do anything she set her mind to. But one of the most important things she taught me was that it is possible for suffering to create a deep compassion and a surprising strength within us. One of her standard phrases was, "I can't bear it . . ." But, in fact, Grandma could bear everything life threw at her, and taught me to do the same.

There was just one thing I disagreed with. Grandma believed in smiling through her pain, in maintaining a happy face no matter what. I made that attitude an unwritten rule of my life. It served me well for a long time, allowing me to soldier on in public, even when things were dreadful at home.

Does any of this sound familiar to you? Have you hidden your scars under a happy face, a pleasing personality, or a polished professional image? Sometimes hiding is the best coping mechanism we have at our disposal.

However, writing the stories of the women in this book became difficult when I realized that I was afraid. I wanted this book to be full of encouragement and I was getting depressed writing it. I could not figure out how to tell these stories in an honest and uplifting way. Then . . .

Boom! That was the problem. This book includes stories from women who could not hide their scars. I was telling very real and honest stories, only some of them with happy endings. It was a trip into the darkness, ironic for someone like me who has never felt very comfortable there.

Pain, suffering, and scarring is unavoidable. There is not a woman alive who has not experienced it. We respond to it differently. Some women hide their pain, like I learned to do, while others wave it as a banner and play the victim card as an excuse for their behavior. And here I was, exploring pain from many different angles, and trying to write about its beauty. No wonder I felt like I was lost in the dark, figuratively and literally. I was going deep into areas that terrified me on purpose! Was I crazy?

Remember when you were a kid and would compare scars? I can remember showing my scabbed knees, skinned elbows, and the scar on my foot where I stepped on a rusty nail. My brothers had cool scars from hitting their heads and falling off a swinging gate. These scars were very apparent when they got their summer buzz haircuts, and they became a conversation piece. It was interesting to see how the skin healed. Sometime a wound left a mark and other times there was a scar.

When did I start hiding my scars?

Isn't that a scary question? I know exactly when it happened to me, and I bet you do too.

We learned to hide the internal scars created from a loss of innocence. Sometimes we decided that our scars said something bad about us and we started to cover them up. I don't know if men do this too, but it seems very common for women. We try to make beautiful something that came from ugliness. If we can't, we hide it deep inside.

These stories have brought pain out of the shadows and put its dark beauty on display. They celebrate courage, survival, and the ability to endure the dark night of the soul. They encourage us to shine a flashlight on things we have covered up and buried so that we can discover how those experiences shaped and honed us. They have removed the shame from scars and have given women the courage to look at them and uncover a nugget of beauty from an unwanted and injuring experience.

If you have read this far in the book, I salute your courage! Thank you for walking with me into the fire and pain, even if we are a little scared. These stories trigger painful memories and bring up things that we don't always want to see, but they're also things that can only be healed when we look at them with new eyes.

Let's hold hands and walk in deeper together. Treasure awaits us and we will find it.

SECTION 3

Cocoon

Arrival

It's quiet on the mountain this morning.

No wind, no birds, silence in the early mist.

When I listen closely, I hear

the river down in the valley,

distant chickens,

a lone truck on the highway.

Life thrums, even when one pays

no attention.

Hope is like that.

In a week of struggle, deep enough

to go unnoticed,

a friend sent trees.

The only one who plants trees

is one who hopes.

Growth takes time.

Resolution requires resting.

But it does arrive,

just like morning and tall trees.

In every Scar Clan story, there comes a point where the woman wants to give up. We all know this dark place – it's hot with anger and frustration, like your face after an ugly cry. It's the place where you just can't see a way to go on. So, you don't.

Instead, you stop, sink down, and let go. You surrender control. You may cry, scoop ice cream or peanut butter directly from the container into your mouth, or you may watch too many hours of mindless television. You may even head to the mall or go online with your credit card in hand, shopping for something that will make you feel better.

Whatever you do, however you cope with the muffled screams that you keep bottled inside, know that you are normal. I call this the cocoon stage of healing. Just like a caterpillar has to go into the dark, dissolve into jelly, and re-form into a butterfly, so do women after scarring.

Surrender. Let go of the idea that you can plan your way out, cry your way out, or even pray your way out. Drop into comfort in whatever way you need it. Reach out to your God, to your best friend, or to a furry animal who loves you, even on the days when you are a hot mess.

I have a 24-hour freak-out rule – when something dreadful happens, I give myself 24 hours to wallow. I'm tender with myself, treating meself as I would treat a child in pain. After that time, something shifts and I start to feel better, perhaps because I took the time to feel the sadness instead of denying it.

When you come to the end of your strength, rest there a while. When we finally give up and let go, healing can arrive. It might look like a red bird on a snowy tree branch or like a miracle that can't be explained. But whatever gift comes to you, treat it as a reminder that you are not alone, and the morning will come after this dark night.

Walking Alone with Grief

I met Martha Giffin at a marketing conference years ago. I was immediately drawn to her bright smile and bubbly personality, and we stayed connected over the years on social media. My heart broke for her when I learned that her youngest son, Ben, had been killed in a car accident coming home from work. He was only twenty-four years old.

Martha had spent the day with her ninety-three-year-old mother, and when Ben called to tell her he was on the way home from work and was looking forward to dinner, Martha said she was too tired to cook but had a pot pie in the freezer he could make when he arrived home. That was their final conversation.

Prior to Ben's death, Martha was bubbly and social, and loved to uplift people. After Ben's death, she was angry, in deep pain, and pulled away from others. She learned that grief is private and very intense. It's a journey she had to walk alone.

Her struggle was so deep that Martha could not find her bearings any longer. She went to a monastery for a silent retreat. Martha loved the slow pace of the days and found it gave her the opportunity to slow down and hear the voice of God. She took slow walks, wrote, and went to evening prayers.

During the retreat, Martha was drawn to a life-sized crucifix. In that moment, she realized that this was the first time in her life she'd deeply suffered and began to be grateful for some of the things she'd been spared. Her son died instantly so she was spared watching him fight for his life. She did not have to make a decision to withdraw life support. Her situation was terrible, but she knew it could have been even worse, and she began to think of others who had lost children to a slow, agonizing death. It was a holy moment, and her spiritual life changed at the foot of that cross. She realized that her purpose in life was going to be bigger and that God was going to use her in a new way.

During her three-year journey with grief, Martha learned the importance of being gentle with herself. She began to notice that she often became jealous when she'd read a post about someone else's child getting married, recovering from an illness or accident, or even seeing posts of family vacations. She began to hate social media.

Ironically, before Ben's accident, Martha was a social media trainer, encouraging business owners to use it effectively. She has a new view of it now.

Social media can be a double-edged sword. It can cause depression and unrest, but it can also connect us to wonderful people. It is important to be aware of who you are connected with, how you feel when you are on social media, and how much time you spend scrolling. There is so much good there, but there is darkness there as well. Today, Martha uses social media as a tool to reach out to others who are grieving. "My friends and followers know my story and how my faith in God was the only thing that helped me after Ben's death. Now, I use social media as a way to share positive and hopeful messages."

Martha learned the value of retreating into a cocoon of quiet while she grieved. Wisely, she did not try to grieve on a schedule or hurry the process. Sometimes, the best gift you can give yourself is a retreat to heal your scars, no matter how long it requires.

Looking in the Mirror

- When you are in pain, how do you retreat from the world?

- Do you get jealous of others whose lives appear to be easier than yours?

"But as for me, I will look to the Lord; I will wait for the God of my salvation; my God will hear me."

- The Bible, Micah 7:7

When Everything Collapses

Like many, Jenn Tasnim got her early scars in childhood, in a home that held danger from alcoholism and emotional abuse. She grew up with no concept of God, but always had a feeling that there was something bigger than she was.

When she was in her early twenties, her boyfriend committed suicide, leaving Jenn with many unanswered questions and deep pain. There was a mystical component to the loss of her beloved that led her to explore spirituality.

She eventually found Sufism, an ancient mystical practice. The poet Rumi was one of the most well-known practitioners of Sufism. Jenn shared, "Sufi means wool. I like the idea that we are wool in the hand of God, being shaped and woven into something beautiful." In Sufi practice, Jenn found comfort and connection to the Divine essence she'd felt all her life. For Jenn, turning to faith was a form of divine restlessness. "I always knew there was something beyond my direct experience and limited perception. It was as if I was a tree whose roots wanted to go deep into something and whose leaves were always turning towards the sun."

Today, Jenn relies on the foundation of her faith to stay centered in a shifting world. When we spoke, it appeared that her life was falling apart. She was in the middle of a divorce, had a cancer diagnosis with an uncertain prognosis, and realized she was failing as a homeschool mom. She loved her two sons deeply and had a fantasy of living on a farm, raising chickens and watching her sons discover the world as she taught them. That fantasy did not play out so well in an apartment in the city, and when she talked with her boys, they were not happy either and wanted to try going to the school down the street.

Instead of beating herself up and feeling like a failure, Jenn agreed with them. "I realized that I could just own the fact that homeschooling was a total train wreck for us and do something else, or I could judge myself as a failure and a rotten mother. The most loving thing to do was to accept that things weren't working and move on."

Now, the boys are thriving in their new school and she is happier working. Jenn also realized that she was asleep in her marriage as well. Nothing terrible was happening, but neither of them were happy. "I could have convinced myself that I needed to give more, to put up with just enough love, and ignore the fact that neither of us was fulfilled. Or, I could be grateful for the years we had, our beautiful sons, and release the relationship in the most loving way possible."

Women have been conditioned to ignore their own happiness, to take it off the table in service of making other people around them happy. We can so easily play the martyr and assume we'll be rewarded for our sacrifice. However, happiness is not a zero-sum equation. Jenn's learned that there is enough happiness for everyone.

"It takes courage to look at life and realize that your happiness matters. I know now that when I am unhappy, it's a message that I need to pay more attention to and be willing to make changes without judgment. Being happy doesn't mean that we are subtracting happiness from others. It just means that we are honoring ourselves, which, in turn, inspires others to strive for their own happiness. That is not a message many women hear when growing up."

Jenn has learned to stay rooted in love and the love of God, the love for others, and the love for herself. This perspective gives her peace, even though she is in a place of uncertainty. "I'm not sure about a lot of things. I don't know how I'll support my boys or what the future holds for my health. It can be scary. But, when I look at the Truth of my life, I can see that I've always been held in Divine love and protection. I've never been outside of God's hands. When life is throwing curve balls, it can be easy to miss the magnificence of Divine Love, but it is always there. I'm trusting in that and waiting."

Jenn's story inspired me. I love to solve problems and find solutions, and I find it difficult to sit in a place of uncertainty. I want to take matters into my own hands and fix them as soon as possible. Jenn's story reminds me that the women of Scar Clan develop a tolerance for situations which cannot be quickly resolved. It takes courage to wait in the cocoon of silence and unknowing.

Looking in the Mirror

- What do you do when your fantasy does not match the reality of your situation?

- How do you care for yourself while you are waiting in the cocoon?

"Where there is ruin, there is hope for a treasure."

- Rumi

Discovering the Difference Between Sadness and Grief

Many of the interviews with the women in this book surprised me. When we started to talk, I was constantly astounded by the depth of their wisdom. This was hard-won wisdom, gained through challenges and surviving some very tough things. I discovered that all women have a wellspring of faith, courage, and knowledge that deepens over her life experiences. You don't need to be an older woman to amass great power, for feminine power comes from the direct experience of life, primarily the painful bits. We learn more from pain than from pleasure, although the pleasure can be much more fun!

Tara lives on an idyllic ranch and uses horses to help others heal. She also has breast cancer and is choosing to heal it naturally. Before her cancer, Tara was acquainted with grief and loss. Like all of us, she's encountered situations of deep pain, but through that pain Tara has discovered that the natural world holds much beauty and healing and she is using that knowledge to help herself and others.

The past few years have been rough for Tara. While she fights off the tumors in her body, she's lost another very close friend to cancer and is a primary caregiver for another friend with cancer. Her family, whom she loves dearly, did not support her choice to forego chemotherapy and use a more holistic and natural approach. Family members and physicians told her she was crazy and would die if she did not follow the standard protocols.

Tara believes that beauty and nature are essential for healing both the body and the heart. She is grateful to live in a rural setting that feels like a sanctuary. When her clients come for workshops, they flourish in the beautiful environment. For more than ten years, Tara's used horses as a personal and spiritual development pathway.

"When people stand near a horse, something magical happens. They learn to be present in the moment, and to release deep emotions that may have been repressed for years. Sometimes, a horse will mirror those repressed emotions so that their human partner can process them."

Horses are deeply intuitive and can read people's emotions easily. When Tara first learned of her tumor, one of her horses came to her and rubbed his head gently up and down her chest, right in the location of the tumor. It felt as if he was lending his support and healing power to that part of her body. Horses have very large hearts, both in a physical and spiritual sense. They are capable of deep feeling. They also forge strong partnerships with people, as long as people set and maintain key boundaries.

Because horses are such large animals, people often feel fearful or intimidated when they stand near them, especially when they are just meeting the animal. Some of Tara's students try to hide their anxiety, but it is reflected back to them by the horse's behavior. "When my participants realize that they are not strange or cowardly because they are nervous around a big horse, they experience a sense of permission and acceptance that is very healing. We just want to know that we are not weird or different from everyone else. It's very comforting to know that others are challenged by some of the same things you are."

As she became more experienced in working with horses as a healing tool, Tara observed that many people carry around repressed grief. Our society tells us that when something happens, we should get past it as quickly as possible, whether that is the death of a loved one or the loss of your health. Tara believes that because society makes us feel like there is something wrong or incorrect about mourning and grief, many people bury it inside where it can fester and cause pain.

She realized that there is a key distinction between grief and sadness. When you end something, like a friendship, career, or even move to a new location, you are sad because a chapter in your life is ending. That sadness will abate over time, primarily because you had a choice in the ending.

Grief is different. You experience grief when something is taken away from you, often without warning. Your husband leaves you for another, your home burns down, you get a terrifying diagnosis; you had no choice in these events. This grief is deep and profound, and it requires time to process and heal.

"Many of us are ashamed of our grief, like it is inconvenient, goes on too long, or is too intense. When someone dies, we get a week or two off from work and then are expected to get back to normal. That is rarely possible, so we put on a brave face and repress our grief, often for many years."

Tara's discovered that grief requires attention and recognition. Whether holding a ceremony in a religious setting or doing something special to recognize and memorialize the loss, when we mark our loss and give ourselves time to mourn it, these rituals can foster great healing.

When you realize that you did not have a choice in a loss, it helps you accept the pain and the time required to heal it. It feels like a healing balm to know that the situation causing your grief was not your choice and, no matter whether you heal that grief quickly or over the course of many years, your response is acceptable.

So, even though Tara is battling cancer and giving great attention to her personal healing, she continues to offer workshops and work with others. "Being around horses is so healing for me. Nature gives us beauty, calm, and perspective. It's important for me to continue to help others, even as I work on my own health. When you are ill or in deep grief, it is very helpful to keep your foot in life as much as possible. Do what you love, help others, and stay connected in any way you can. That connection is a powerful healing tool."

Life is a series of challenges that are designed to help us grow. We don't always like the lessons. No one wants to have cancer, lose a loved one, or face a terrifying challenge. Tara's learned that, in those situations, it is important to be kind to yourself and others, and over time, she's learned to trust herself, even when others vehemently protest her decisions.

"We have a common thread of humanity that unites us all. We all grapple with vulnerability, grief, and pain. There is no "perfect way" to respond when we are faced with unexpected loss. Just knowing that everyone faces these challenges helps us to accept our own process and the time it requires. For me, I trust myself to make good choices, spend as much time in beauty and the natural world as I can, and I continue to help others. These actions give me peace and power to face whatever comes my way."

The idea of belonging to the Scar Clan, a tribe of women who have suffered, waited for solutions, and discovered ways to transcend pain, gives me great comfort. Many of us feel strange or different. The good news is that we are all the same! Every woman has scars. The women who inspire me, like Tara, are those who have found peace and power as they transcend the circumstances of their lives.

Looking in the Mirror

- How do you use beauty and nature to support your peace of mind?

- When you read Tara's belief that grief is caused from something that was not your choice, what did you feel?

"Out of suffering have emerged the strongest souls; the most massive characters are seared with scars."

- Khalil Gibran

Holding on to Hope

Anna, her husband, and their three children were happily living in Texas when life began to change. Anna had finally found peace of mind after a very challenging youth and was happy in her role as a pastor's wife. Her parents were good people who did the best they could, but her father had severe PTSD, so growing up at home was difficult for Anna and her siblings.

Faith has always been important to Anna. "I feel like God picked me up by the nape of my neck when I was a child and kept me close ever since." She attended Bible college, met her husband at church, and has always prayed. People often told her she would be a great minister, but she felt her role was to support her husband in his ministry instead. When she was thirty, she had an experience that changed her mind.

Anna and her husband were working at a Christian youth camp. One night, all the teens walked up a mountain by torchlight for a special service. When Anna was at the top of that mountain, God spoke to her, telling her she was already ministering and needed to have the training and recognition of her denomination. Anna wasn't sure but obeyed the call she received and spent the next five years in an ordination program.

As soon as she graduated, Anna had a cancer scare that required six months of careful attention to her health. Then her mother, who lived in the Midwest, was diagnosed with cancer, and Anna went back and forth as often as she could. But while they prayed and prayed for healing, her mother's cancer was aggressive, and fifteen months later, she died.

It was a very dark time for Anna. Her grief was deep as she prepared for her ordination. She mourned that her mother, who had also been an ordained minister, would not be there to see her reach that important goal. She did the only thing she could do and moved forward.

Shortly after her ordination, Anna's husband felt they should co-pastor a church in the Midwestern state where she grew up. Anna had so many painful memories that she did not want to return there, but they prayed about it both separately and as a family and started to interview with congregations there.

One week after a very positive interview, Anna learned that her older brother was injured in a terrible shop fire. He was burned over much of his body and his heart, lungs, and kidneys were failing. He spent four months in intensive care and an additional six months in the hospital before being discharged. Anna and her husband were offered the co-pastoring job and moved during this time, but they drove their moving truck right to the hospital to sit with her brother before doing anything else.

It was a very difficult time to begin a new career. However, the members of their new church were incredibly supportive. Anna felt like God gave her a message; a word of comfort and the right inspiration every time she was at the end of her rope.

When her brother was ready to be discharged, he had nowhere to go, because his wife ended their marriage while he was in the hospital. He was in a wheelchair, needed constant care, and had very few motor skills. He moved in with Anna's dad, but it was a difficult situation. Anna's father was a hoarder, was very stubborn and had uneasy relationships with all of his children. Anna tried to help. When she visited, she'd clean and encourage her father to let go of some of his possessions, but he was unwilling to do so.

Six months later, the two men were out one day when her father drove into a stopped car, while he was travelling 70 miles per hour in a construction zone on the highway. He hit a family of three who all perished in the crash, while her brother had a broken sternum and her father was critically injured.

Anna immediately drove six hours to the hospital. Her father's situation was very grave. He was on a ventilator and in a coma most of the time, but he did wake up long enough to make peace with his youngest children, who just happened to be present on the day he was able to speak. He had a serious head wound and his blood pressure was dropping. Further testing revealed that he also was suffering from dementia and Stage Four liver cancer.

After six days, the care team and family had to decide whether or not to remove life support. Everyone looked to Anna, the eldest daughter, to make the decision. She prayed and prayed for wisdom and for a sign, and when the voting came, it was a unanimous decision to end the suffering and remove life support.

Anna was left with a mountain of problems to manage. Her younger siblings were not able to cope, and her older brother was disabled and in the hospital. She had to navigate her brother's care, his divorce, and she had to get him into the VA system for ongoing care.

The car accident killed four people and created numerous expenses that far exceeded the limits of her father's insurance. Her father's house was crammed full of junk and had to be prepared for sale. Anna had five attorneys on retainer in three different states. Just addressing all the paperwork was overwhelming in and of itself.

There was more. Anna and her family had been restoring a beautiful old house for the past two years. The renovations were completed when Anna was sitting in the hospital with her father. They loved their home but realized that it would be impossible for them to care for her brother in that house. So, they put it on the market and purchased a more accessible house a few blocks away, and now they had two mortgages on top of all their other expenses. Soon, her disabled brother came to live with them, and he needed constant attention, feeding, and almost total care of his body.

At this point in the interview, I asked Anna how she had the strength to endure all this pressure, raise three teens, and co-pastor a church. She told me that she could not survive without God. Her life has never been easy, so, many years ago, she established a practice of spending an hour every morning with her Lord. That spiritual time is her lifeline.

She's also been washed in support by members of her congregation and community. She shared, "I could easily frame the story of my life as one of suffering and trials. However, I refuse to do that. God is good and we are meant to live in joy. When my mom was dying, I read a book that encouraged me to find a gift in every situation. I've held onto that idea over these past painful years. I'm still going to smile and be grateful for what God has given me. My problems are far from over. I'm in the midst of a storm right now. Some days I don't know how I can cope with the attorneys, insurance companies, bills, and feeding my older brother. I have not learned great wisdom or become angelic. But, every day, God gives me a word, an insight, or a message of love. It's like manna and it keeps me going."

Anna often feels alone and knows that few can understand the pressures she is facing. "The phone rings forty times every day with someone wanting something. I'm juggling so many things that it is a miracle I can remember my own name. I used to pray that God would give me more of Him and less of me. That's a dangerous prayer, but it is being answered. My faith sustains me, and I see evidence of God's care every day."

There is a scripture that says, "God comforts us so that we can comfort others." This verse has sustained Anna for the past five years. At times she feels guilty for having all these problems and wonders if people in her church would prefer a minister with a more normal life. However, they tell her that her story gives them hope and comfort.

Anna is grateful for her family, her congregation, and God's faithfulness. "Even on days when I want to give up, something happens that gives me a sense of renewal and hope. I'm clear that suffering is limited and, someday, I'll be free of these burdens, even if it is when I enter heaven. My mother named me Anna after the woman in the Bible who waited patiently for her Savior. Mom also prayed daily that I would become a pillar of faith. Knowing that, I can find the strength to move forward, one step at a time. I pray that my brother will recover, that we can sell both my father's house and our house, that all the legal dealings will end, and that I can continue to be the wife, mother, and minister I want to be. I am far from perfect, but I have learned how to wait patiently for the Lord, just like my namesake."

It is hard to imagine one woman enduring all these trials. Anna's decision to keep her eyes on joy and gratefulness, instead of giving in to despair, is a powerful witness to faith. Whether you identify with a particular religious tradition or spiritual practice or not, you can nurture faith while you are waiting for deliverance. It's not my business to tell you what to believe. Instead, my encouragement is for you to believe in something that gives you peace. My experience, like Anna's, tells me that faith is a cornerstone of hope and healing.

Looking in the Mirror

- How do you frame the stories of your scars?

- After reading Anna's story and how she refuses to focus on her suffering, do you feel inspired to make any changes to your stories?

"I've decided to meet destiny with as much good cheer and as little drama as I can- because how I choose to handle myself is entirely my own choice. My ultimate choice is always to approach my work from a place of stubborn gladness."

- Elizabeth Gilbert

If you are deep in the cocoon of pain, I urge you to look towards the future while giving yourself permission to wait as long as you need to grieve and heal at your own pace. The Scar Clan women recognize your suffering, grief, and pain. Recovery will take grit and a stubborn refusal to stay stuck in your cocoon, but you will emerge more beautiful and stronger than before.

SECTION 4

Change

Someone I loved once gave me a box full of darkness. It took me years
to understand that this too, was a gift.   – Mary Oliver

You know that feeling of disgust and discontent that creeps up over you? It usually arrives when you've been ignoring the truest voice of your soul, living out the expectations of others by keeping the peace. Whether you are in a job you don't like, a relationship that is slowly eroding your joy and self-respect, or you've put up with a problem that isn't getting any better, there will come a day when you just cannot and will not take it anymore.

This is a holy day.

Your feelings of disgust, anger, and irritation are signs that you must make a change. You realize you can't wait any longer for the other person to stop bullying you, for the economy to improve, or to have that nagging health challenge disappear.

On this holy day, you take a stand for YOU. You are finally so uncomfortable that you are willing to take steps to move, to quit, or to speak your truth. Thomas Edison said that discontent is the first necessity of progress. He was right. We only change when we get so disgusted that we are willing to take action.

And this disgust is at work, not just in our personal lives, but collectively. Women are frustrated with the state of the world – the pollution, the harm to the vulnerable, the injustice, the lies. We rise to speak out, to lend a hand, or to support a cause that is important to the future.

Any growth, personally and globally, begins when a woman says "Enough!" and decides to make a change.

Be grateful for discontent, disgust, and disquiet. They are catalysts of great power.

The stories in this section all focus on the decision to make a change, to say no to a life of pain and aim for something better.

Running Away Toward Home

From 2008 onward, I had trouble sleeping. My life was a mass of dreadful stress and I couldn't shut my mind off at night. Counting sheep didn't work, so I started a practice of imagining beautiful homes where I could live.

I would see each room in detail, selecting furnishings, colors, and the outdoor environment. It was very relaxing to consider what type of curtains would be on the kitchen windows and what kind of view they framed. I designed many imaginary houses, but my favorite was a one-story with cathedral ceilings, an open floor plan, huge kitchen, and a covered front porch. I could see myself sitting on the porch writing with a golden retriever at my feet.

By 2011, my life was getting worse. My father, brother, and mother all had cancer at the same time. Mom hung on, but Dad and David died. I knew that stress exacerbated cancer, and my intuition told me I was next if I did not take serious steps to change my life. Years before, I considered moving to Ecuador when I retired, but even at fifty years old I worried I wouldn't make it to retirement. It was time for a radical change, and Ecuador offered me the opportunity to do so.

When I decided to seriously consider moving to Ecuador, I registered for a real estate tour in Cuenca, a beautiful city high in the Andes. On the final day of the tour, we drove out of the city for about an hour to a beautiful valley near the small town of Paute. There was a river running through the valley and amazing mountain vistas. The first stop was at a house offered for sale by US owners. When I walked in, I almost fainted. It was the house I made up in my head, complete with the big kitchen, porch, and cathedral ceilings. I desperately wanted it, but the price was far above my price range. It seemed like a cruel trick to see the house I'd created in my imagination years ago and not being able to afford it.

Then we went to our final stop, about four miles away, to a vacant lot on a mountainside with an amazing view. There was nothing on the land except trees and a mud hut where someone was squatting. I got very dizzy. As soon as we got out of the van, I heard a voice in my head saying, "This is where you will live." I got even dizzier and felt about to faint. I thought I had altitude sickness or I was losing my marbles.

The lot was about an acre, long and thin, stretching from the top of the mountain across the road and down to a ravine. Parts of it were very steep, but the site where the mud hut sat was a perfect site with an amazing view of the valley below.

I felt very strange. There was a sensation of strong desire in me, almost like lust. I wanted that land desperately. I spoke with the tour guide, Xavier, who was also a realtor, and I learned that he purchased the property from the neighbors and planned to build on it, but his wife did not want to live in such a remote location. He sold it to his architect friend, Pablo, who had already designed a house plan for the lot. Then, Xavier told me that Pablo had built the house I'd looked at earlier. I asked if it would be possible for Pablo to build that house with the big porch on this lot instead of the house he'd planned. I was shaking with fear and excitement. This was crazy but something kept urging me onward.

Things started to move very quickly. After we returned to Cuenca at the end of the tour, Xavier took me to Pablo's office. I liked them both so much. They seemed like trustworthy, caring people. We all talked about the possibilities, and by the end of the meeting, Pablo agreed to construct the house of my dreams on the mountain lot.

I was terrified. It was a big investment and would have to be a cash purchase as mortgages are rare in Ecuador. I could pay it off over the twelve-month building period but had no idea where I could get the money. This was in the midst of the real estate crash in the USA and I was underwater with my home in St. Louis. While Pablo determined pricing, I had time to think about it overnight, so I spent a sleepless night wrestling with this crazy idea. I was seriously considering moving to South America! I had no idea how I could do this, where the money would come from, or what my family would say.

The next day, I went to the Cathedral in the center of Cuenca and prayed. I was there for hours wrestling with my desire. I told God that if I was to go through with this idea, I needed to have a clear sign. I asked for a feeling of peace if I was to move forward. I was so nervous and erratic that I knew that any feeling of peace would be an unmistakable sign. I waited, I felt that peace, but I didn't trust it. So, I asked again and doubted the answer yet again. After the third request, that feeling of peace resisted my attempts to wipe it away with my fear. Yikes! I called Xavier and asked him to make an offer on the property.

The real estate process in Ecuador is very different from what I was accustomed to. Your realtor does all negotiations on your behalf without you. Xavier asked me what my top price would be, exactly what I wanted, and then he arranged a tour of Ingaprica, an archeological site about two hours away.

The following day I did the tour and loved seeing the Incan ruins, llamas, and beautiful haciendas. The tour took all day. When I returned to Cuenca at about 4pm, Xavier called. Pablo agreed to build the house I wanted on that lot at the price I wanted. If I wanted to move forward, I needed to make a $2000 cash deposit immediately and sign a contract to pay the rest of the money over the next twelve months. Xavier would pick me up the next morning and introduce me to his cousin, Diego, an attorney who could handle the contracts and help me with my residency paperwork.

This was getting so real! I went to an ATM and started the process of gathering the money, all in twenty-dollar bills. It had to be done over two days. I was terrified to have so much cash on me in a foreign country, but I was grateful for my money belt and my chubby belly that disguised the wad of cash around my middle. When I arrived at the attorney's office, I was in such a dither that I could not count the money. I tried to just put it in piles of ten but couldn't even do that. I will never forget pushing that big pile of bills across the desk to Diego and asking him to make sure it was all there. He was very kind.

The deal was done, and I returned to St. Louis the next day. Three months later, my husband, son, and I arrived in Ecuador with two suitcases each, ready to start our new life.

Everyone thought I was crazy. My sons were unhappy about losing their childhood home and the possessions stored there. It was wrenching to sell everything, including all my beloved books. I cried when we sold the Christmas decorations at our garage sale, but we sold it all. I cleaned out my bank accounts and retirement fund to make the first payments on the property.

Fast forward three years, there I was – living on my mountain, writing on that front porch, just like in my dream. Miraculously, all the money arrived just in the nick of time and the house was mine. There were many rocky moments during those three years, including the crumbling of my marriage. I struggled to master Spanish and adjust to a new culture, and because I was the only expat in our small community, I was a curiosity, taller and bigger than all of the women and most of the men. I made many mistakes and laughed a lot. Thankfully, people were very accepting and kind.

After a couple of years, my son returned to the United States to begin his career and I was living alone for the first time in twenty-seven years. One day, my friend Linda called from the nearby village. I had previously told her the story of how I dreamed of my current house many years ago, and Linda had called to tell me about a golden retriever puppy she saw up for adoption. I raced into town and adopted Millie, who is sleeping nearby as I write this. The vision was complete, eight years after I created it.

I've lived in my house on the mountain for almost seven years now with my rescue dogs, Millie and Clifford. I start each day with the dogs on the porch, sipping tea and writing in my journal. I look around and marvel that I am living in a picture I created in my head that seemed like just a fantasy. I am happy, healthy, and surrounded by good friends. My neighbors have adopted me into their family, where I serve as a godmother and the official cake cutter at family celebrations. My sons are doing well in the United States and we've found ways to stay close, even with the many miles between us. There have been many miracles in my life, but this is the most amazing one so far. I came to Ecuador a stressed out, unhappy woman, desperate for a better life. And then I found the home of my heart, in a place I'd never expected, but I knew it was right the moment I saw it.

Honestly, I don't think I would have been brave enough to make this momentous change without my scars. Moving to Ecuador was a challenge, but not as hard as what I'd already endured.

There is an unexpected benefit to surviving deep wounds. You have a measuring stick. You know what you've overcome. Ever after, you can say, "Well, this is hard, but not as bad as what I've already faced." That resilience will travel with you for the rest of your life, giving you power and strength, and it grows with every additional risk you take or sorrow you transcend. The women of Scar Clan never stop developing and deepening their courage. Then, there will come a day when you reach out a hand to help a sister in need. You can become a mentor and an inspiration, because you changed, and you are stronger because of it.

Looking in the Mirror

- How do you use the power of your intuition?

- Describe the holy day when you decided to stop putting up with pain in your life and chose to change:

"If you're one of those people who has that little voice in the back of her mind saying, 'Maybe I could do [fill in the blank],' don't tell it to be quiet. Give it a little room to grow, and try to find an environment it can grow in."

- Reese Witherspoon

Change or Die

Diagnosed with Type 1 diabetes when she was in her final semester of graduate school, Amelia Buschena was twenty-six and an oddity. Type 1 diabetes is usually diagnosed in childhood, so it was rare for it to go unnoticed for so long. She'd been quite sick for about a year and no one could determine the source of the problem, but during a holiday vacation at her new husband's family farm, she got very ill and visited a clinic. Her fasting blood sugar was 250, and the doctor told her to go immediately to the hospital. Her first question after her diagnosis was if she could still have children.

Amelia's life changed in that moment. Up to then, she'd been a very healthy, free-spirited person who loved to be spontaneous. Now she needed to count every carbohydrate, to always carry sugar with her, and to plan everything out ahead of time. She heard the words, "Manageable, not treatable," and realized she'd never get better.

The learning curve was steep. There was so much new information, and it was a constant struggle to balance her levels of exercise, food intake, and rest. She had to learn how to administer insulin shots four times each day just to stay alive.

She realized she had a choice. She could learn to live well with her new condition, or she could get angry, rebel, and die. The choice was clear.

Amelia was sad and angry. She had always taken care of her health and did all she had to do, but she was really upset. She'd been planning on enjoying her final semester of graduate school, celebrating her accomplishments and concentrating on her projects, while enjoying her new husband. She never expected a health crisis that could end her life.

But Amelia's faith was strong, and she was getting a degree in theology. She latched on to the biblical story of the paralyzed man whose friends took the roof off a building to get him in front of Jesus. So, Amelia turned to friends and her husband for support.

Her support team did everything they could to uplift her. They helped her learn how to cook, sat with her when she experienced low blood sugar, and prayed with her. These friends, her family, and her faith helped Amelia release her anger and adjust to her new life.

"I believe that everything happens for a reason with but I could not see the reason that God gave me diabetes. However, I know God can handle my complaints and periodic pouting. In time, I started to see that my situation was challenging and difficult, but, with support, I could manage it successfully. God gives us a community, friends and family who can pick us up when we are unable to stand, and they help us return to joy."

Amelia believes that it is important to acknowledge all of your feelings, the pleasant and unpleasant ones. Denying them is not healthy. "Some days I don't have to think twice about my diabetes. Other days, something new happens and I'll have to make adjustments. When my blood sugar gets really low, I can't really speak. My brain doesn't work, and it feels scary. Now I have an insulin pump and that's made my life much easier. At first, I used to bump it and it felt odd. Now, it's just how I do life, a part of me.

"I never considered death much before. When I learned that I had a disease that could lead to my death at twenty-six, my life changed. I learned that it is important to bring as much joy as possible into every day."

Today, Amelia and her husband co-pastor a church and are the parents of an adorable little girl. Because of her diabetes, there were risks during her pregnancy, but the couple met with her endocrinologist and then her obstetrician to talk about those risks and strategies for a successfully not pregnancy. It was important for her to tightly control her blood sugar, even before conception, to decrease the risk of birth defects for the baby and to keep Amelia healthy.

The pregnancy was challenging and had some scary moments. Her blood sugars were very uneven no matter what she ate. Amelia developed pre-eclampsia and required constant medical monitoring, but after much worry, and 42 hours of labor, a healthy baby girl, Gwendolyn, was delivered at 36 weeks. Her name was chosen because it means "blessed".

"Because my pregnancy was challenging, it means so much to me that my body was able to bring a child into the world. My community, the doctor, my family, and friends gave me a tremendous amount of support. There are things I had to give up and change, but having a baby was something that I could do. I am so thankful. Even the congregation where we work got involved. They adopted us and brought meals and provided an incredible level of support. I believe people are created for community. We don't always realize that we have people around us who make up our community until we need them. It took a strong community to help me adjust to diabetes, find a way to live a regular life, and have a child. I am incredibly blessed and thankful."

I am grateful that Amelia married my nephew, Andrew, so that I had the opportunity to witness the way she dealt with her life-changing diagnosis. She is a woman of deep faith and abundant joy. Amelia's story shows us that we don't have to walk alone. When we are brave enough to ask for help, people will respond. Sometimes, help comes from those closest to us. Other times, family and friends are unable to give us what we need, and new friends arrive who step into the gap. When you're put into a situation in which you know that you must change, reach out and catch the hands of those who will support and celebrate you.

Looking in the Mirror

- Describe the community of support you have around you now.

- How do you support other people in your community?

"The glory of friendship is not the outstretched hand, nor the kindly smile, nor the joy of companionship; it is the spiritual inspiration that comes to one when you discover that someone believes in you and is willing to trust you with a friendship."

\- R.W. Emerson

Brave Enough to Ask

Felicia works as a professional speaker. She speaks to business and professional groups all around the world on a variety of motivational and training subjects. She loves her work and she's good at it.

Five years ago, she started to feel strange when she took a deep breath. There was no pain or other problems, but it felt like there was something in her lungs. After visiting her physician, she was shocked to learn she had lung cancer at age forty-two, despite having no risk factors. She'd never smoked, worked around other smokers, asbestos, or radon. But then she learned that there are three kinds of lung cancer: small cell, non-small cell, and this very rare kind that no one talks about much. Hers was small cell and required surgery. She was shocked and frightened.

Felicia is a woman of great faith, although she doesn't really talk about it much, preferring to live her life as a quiet witness to her beliefs. However, on the night before her surgery, she was inspired to send an email out to her list and post on social media. Her request said, "If you are the praying kind, please pray. If you are the visualizing kind, please visualize. If you are into energy, please send all the good vibes you can. I am having surgery tomorrow for lung cancer. Please pray." This message went out to more than 30,000 people around the world.

When Felicia woke from her surgery, her doctor was there. The doctor said that she'd never seen anything like this before. Her biopsy had clearly shown small cell lung cancer. However, once the surgery started, the team found something else – that very rare kind of cancer, mucoepidermoid. This cancer was so rare that a twenty-year study by Harvard University found only twelve people diagnosed with it. They all survived and required no additional treatment after surgery. Her doctor said, "I don't know what happened, but overnight you had a miracle."

Felicia credits the prayers of people all around the world with her miracle. It was almost overwhelming to receive so much support from people she'd never met. She received many beautiful messages, people asked their friends and faith communities to pray for her, and she experienced a medical miracle. Like so many women, Felicia is strong, independent, and much more apt to give support than to receive it.

For a time after her surgery, Felicia had trouble speaking and would cough violently every few seconds, making it impossible for her to do her job as a professional speaker. She wondered if she should find a different profession or go to work for a corporation. Yet, when she prayed about it, she heard that speaking was her gift and she would continue to serve the world in that way. Over time, her coughing and voice problems healed, and she was able to resume her speaking career, including sharing the story of her miraculous healing.

When Felicia tells this story today in her presentations, people are very moved, even in serious business settings. She has gotten standing ovations and has noticed people in tears. She'd never been shy about her faith before, but now she was even more comfortable talking about miracles and the power of asking for help.

"I learned to not be afraid of sharing personal challenges. So many people try to hide challenges and difficulties. When I was in a stressful situation and shared it, I was flooded with support and I truly believe that support made a powerful difference. Everyone has pain, hardships, challenges, and problems. When we are brave enough to share them and ask for help, people step up in amazing ways.

"I had lung cancer for three weeks. After asking for support, it was gone. I can't explain it in any other way than to say all those people praying, visualizing, and sending me energy created a miracle. That's what can be possible when you ask."

It can be scary to ask for help. It can be even more frightening when you are in a professional situation. Many of us have faced discrimination in the workplace, and while it might not be as pronounced as what happened to our mothers and grandmothers if they worked outside the home, every woman has a story about a time when she was treated differently because of her gender. Whether it was being passed over for promotion, being paid less than your male counterparts, or fending off unwanted advances, you know the sting. Many professional women build an armor of independence, striving to appear competent and in control at all times. It can be a wise survival mechanism.

But when Felicia stopped pretending that she was invincible and asked for help in a very public way, miracles occurred. Not only was she healed, she learned that she could safely show her vulnerability and, as a token of that, an unwavering confidence in her career. Women of the Scar Clan know that asking for help is not a weakness; it's a tremendous show of strength.

Looking in the Mirror

- When have you been brave enough to ask for support?

- How have you been surprised by support from others?

"Asking for help with shame says: You have the power over me. Asking with condescension says: I have the power over you. But asking for help with gratitude says: We have the power to help each other."

- Amanda Palmer

You Can Do Anything, It Just Might Take Longer

Sally was born in a Mississippi small town many years ago. She was diagnosed with cerebral palsy at birth.

Back then, there were no therapies or support services available, but Sally's pediatrician told her mother that if Sally could learn how to ride a horse, she might learn how to walk as well. Sally went to a summer camp for four years and learned how to ride, winning second place in the camp horse show when she was eight. Up to that point, it was the proudest moment of her life.

"My mom was determined that I would be okay. She taught me that I could figure out how to do anything I wanted to do, even if it took a little longer than the other kids." Sally learned how to swim and ride her bike, but it took a long time.

Their community was surrounded by pecan trees and Sally wanted to climb the trees like other kids. She'd sneak out at night to practice. Her legs were not strong enough to climb, so she learned to use her arms. "My mother was a Southern Belle and she was horrified that I'd develop huge biceps and look terrible in my debutante gown, but she let me climb." Little Sally got into trouble when she teased the boys that only sissies used their legs to climb a tree. After two of them broke their arms, she had to stop taunting them.

The town was so small that Sally knew all of her classmates from nursery school onward. "No one ever bothered me about my walking until a new boy moved to town in second grade and started calling me names. My friends joined in and I was devastated. That was the first time I realized that having cerebral palsy was going to cause me some problems."

However, that wasn't her only problem. Her father was an alcoholic and had a mistress. Everyone in town liked him because he was a happy drunk and a good attorney. Sally could tell that he was embarrassed by her disability, and then her mother suddenly developed a drinking problem as well.

By the time Sally was in high school, she continued in the family tradition of heavy drinking. When Sally was eighteen, her beloved older brother was killed in Vietnam and the family disintegrated. "I stayed drunk for about the next three years. I got married too young and had two babies before I was twenty-two. Things got really out of hand and my pediatrician threatened to have social services take my kids away if I didn't stop drinking. I went to my first AA meeting that day and have been sober ever since."

Her first years of sobriety were hard. It took about five years for her to feel settled internally. And then, she realized she was gay. "I didn't think it would be a big deal to tell my parents, so I announced what I discovered about myself. My father was a judge by then and absolutely furious. He told me he'd take my kids away and I'd never see them again." They disowned her. "I don't think my parents ever thought I'd be able to support myself and my children. If they hadn't kicked me out of the family, I might have stayed dependent on them forever. Sometimes, the people who hurt you the most give you the greatest gift of your life."

Sally ran away with her two children and stayed with a friend in Nebraska, thinking no one would ever look for her there. She'd never had a job and now had to figure out how to provide for herself and her children. This all was happening at a time when computers were brand new in the workplace, so Sally took a computer course and discovered a knack for programming. She enrolled in a six-month certification computer course, graduated, and went on to a very successful career in computer programing.

Sally was always scared. She was so nervous during her first months as a computer programmer that she'd throw up every day before work. However, she realized that she couldn't wait to feel confident; she had to just do what she could when she was scared. "In my mind I was still this chubby little kid with a gimpy leg. How could some business trust me with their computers?" She thought that if she just had a normal body, life would be fine.

That thinking changed when she met a woman in AA who was a great softball player. She was jealous. Sally went to one of her games, saw her hit a home run and was shocked when the woman committed suicide two days later. She discovered that everyone gets scared; it wasn't just her problem.

Today, Sally is happily married to Vickie, the love of her life. Retired from her successful career, she loves to scuba dive and spend time with her children and grandchildren. She wakes up amazed at her life. "I learned that you don't have to be special. I'm pretty ordinary, but I've had the opportunity to do extraordinary things. All you have to do is make the best of what you've got. When you are heartbroken or overwhelmed, don't give up. Just do the next thing that makes sense. In time you'll figure it out. There is always a way around every challenge."

I'm lucky to have Sally as my friend. Her sense of humor and unstoppable attitude inspire everyone who meets her, not because they feel sorry about her medical condition, but because she's fun. Sally, and other women who have transcended many painful things, develop a non-judgmental manner that welcomes others. When your pain has taken you to the bottom of life, you develop a sensitivity towards others who struggle, along with the confidence that you can work around whatever life throws at you next.

Looking in the Mirror

- Who gave you a gift when they hurt you?

- How did that scarring lead you forward in life?

"Take chances, make mistakes. That's how you grow. Pain nourishes your courage. You have to fail in order to practice being brave."

- Mary Tyler Moore

SECTION 5

Create

"Every great dream begins with a dreamer. Always remember, you have within you the strength, the patience, and the passion to reach for the stars to change the world."

— Harriet Tubman

Grandmothers know how to mend. They know how to take something that appears to be useless and create something beautiful from it.

Mending is a woman's skill that can easily be overlooked, like most powerful magic. Women learn to make soup from burned meals, to turn a torn blouse into a quilt block or transform a failure at work into a learning opportunity. We may not mend our socks any longer, but members of the Scar Clan know how to mend a broken life.

Our culture made us believe that throwing things away was best. We were rich because we could discard things and people. It was easy to get a replacement, whether it was a pair of shoes with worn soles or a new friend. We giggled at our depression-born grandmothers who saved buttons, plastic bags, and balls of string.

When I moved to Ecuador, I met women who mended. Clothing is expensive here, so it is carefully maintained. Shoes are polished and resoled. Garden scraps are used to feed animals. Nothing is wasted.

So too is our life. Nothing is wasted. Every misstep or failure is our teacher. When we get another scar, over time we weave those tattered edges of our lives back together. We can create a beautiful life, no matter how many scars, fears, or wounds we carry. Now that I am closer to the end of my life than the beginning, I can look back and see that the mended parts of my life became the most beautiful.

The Power of Grace

I grew up in the Lutheran Church. There are several varieties of Lutherans, like flavors of ice cream. My family was from the strict German branch and we were woven tightly into that wood. One of my ancestors studied with Martin Luther himself back in the 1600s, and another was a famous minister who led groups of earnest German immigrants to St. Louis where he wrote books and founded the first seminary. My mother taught in Lutheran schools before she married, and we attended church events without question. Up until the 8th grade, I attended a Lutheran school that my grandparents helped build, and I loved it. Our brand of faith appealed to my bookish sense, and we believed that the answer to every question was in "The Book", the Holy Bible, the inspired word of God. I went to a Lutheran college, became a Lutheran schoolteacher, and spent a few years working for the church.

However, I was a fraud. I didn't agree with some of the tenets of the church, and I so wanted to be a pastor, but that was forbidden because I was a female. I did not warm to the cold judgment present in some of the church members, many of which who were sure that they were just a little more right than other Christians. If my family had been a different flavor of Lutheran or even a different type of Protestant, I could have been a pastor leading people to God. I had the skillset and would have been good at it. It seemed like a cruel trick.

There were also a few things about Martin Luther, and my ancestor, CFW Walther, that were troubling. They were men of their times and reflected the cultural bias against women and others who did not fit their ideas of what was right and wrong. And then there was me, a bleeding-heart liberal, born into one of the most conservative churches in the world.

Yet, I am so grateful to them and everyone who helped shape my faith as I was growing up. I learned to study and really think about faith instead of just accepting what I was taught. Lutherans are cerebral, with strong values, and a love of tradition and ritual, and I loved being part of a chain of believers who did the same thing on Sunday, no matter where they were in space and time. I also learned that the local congregations set the tone for where they fell on the meter of conservatism, and I knew I could find a place that suited me.

However, the most important thing I learned in Sunday School and Bible college, as well in the classroom and from the pulpit, was the concept of grace – the love that swoops in just when you need it, not because you did anything to deserve it, but because God loves you just as you are.

Grace is a miracle to me. So much of my twisted thinking focuses on earning – earning love, respect, attention, and even safety. I was raised to be the very best good girl I could be: kind, helpful, cheerful, good at school, chaste, respectful and someone who would make my parents and my God proud of me.

Yet, while I worked hard to do that, I always fell short. I talked back to my mother, gossiped with my friends, and asked adults impertinent questions just to show off. Then, when I became an adult, I got divorced twice, harbored deep anger and resentment, and raised wild, naughty little boys who caused trouble and were noisy in church. I failed miserably and felt like no one would love me, least of all, God.

I'll always be astonished by the grace I was given. My parents told me I was right to leave my scary, dangerous husband. My Lutheran pastor told me God did not create me to suffer and that divorce was the wisest course of action in my circumstances. Church members were kind and welcoming. I was not shamed or burned at the stake. Turns out I was the only one judging me harshly. I was bathed in grace and support from unexpected sources.

Whether or not you grew up in a church, you grew up with ideas about earning love. We were all taught we had to be a certain way to be worthy of love from a husband, from others, and from the Divine. It didn't matter who we were naturally – we all needed tidying and polishing to be acceptable. It took constant effort not to become too much of any one thing – too fat, too loud, too old, or too anything that threatened others or called attention to ourselves.

This goes back to early history. Women were vulnerable back in the hunter gatherer days. If you were cast out of the cave, you'd be cold, hungry, and likely dinner for something with big teeth. Furthermore, throughout history, women have been traded as possessions. The pretty ones were valuable for strategic marriages or as mistresses of important men. The plain ones had to be hard workers, good mothers, or entered convents where they could excel in studies, prayers, or service. None of those roads were easy, and, even now, women feel the threat of being cast out of the tribe. Today, that might show up as a fear of losing your job, marriage or home, but the fear of being cold and alone still haunts many of us.

And yet, it is changing. In my lifetime, I've seen women embrace themselves, celebrate who they are, and lessen their focus on earning love. We are starting to realize that we are love, and that God, in whatever name we use, loves us just as we are. We are starting to feel safer and more able to care for ourselves with or without a man or institution to protect us. The chains of the patriarchy are loosing, and little girls are no longer taught to hide their intelligence, anger, or power in order to find a boy who will date them.

This is grace. We are finally getting to the point where we can own ourselves, our scars, and our talents, powers, and flaws. We now know we are worthy of love, both from ourselves and others. The problem is not solved, but it is beginning. The world my granddaughter is coming into is both better and worse than the one I grew up in. There are more opportunities for women, and more problems to be solved.

There is also the need for more grace, as well as more acceptance of ourselves and for others. I learned that I am more judgmental and crueler to myself than anyone else has ever been, but I'm working on changing that and have made good progress. I believe in grace, in love, and in miracles because I've tasted them, both from other people and from the Divine. I've been saved from danger on more than one occasion. I've learned other people will step in to help, that I have a strength and resilience I never expected, and that God is always over my shoulder, ready to love me in the midst of my messy life.

Divine love never stops, I just can't see it all the time when my vision gets clouded by my fear and judgment. I'm evolving in my understanding of grace and my ability to give it to myself and others. I'll never get it perfectly right, because perfection is not possible here on Earth. But I'm growing into more love and less judgment, more grace and less distance. I've learned that grace and love are present in many churches, faith traditions, and even in those who don't use the word God at all but have a sense of the Divine that is as deep as mine. I've met people who welcomed and accepted me without even knowing me or all my scars and dramas, recognizing something in my eyes that they warmed to, even though we did not speak the same language. Life is a miracle, filled with moments of pain and grace that take my breath away.

I don't claim to understand it. Yet, when I watch a hawk soar over my valley, when I see the sunset over the ocean, or when I touch the hand of another, I know we are all more than we think we are, more loved, and that nature never stops showing us the majesty of Divine grace.

Looking in the Mirror

- Did you struggle with the feeling that you had to earn love, respect, or safety like I did?

- In what ways can you begin to give yourself more grace – the love you don't have to earn?

"Faith is a living, daring, confidence in God's grace."

- Martin Luther

Just a One-Way Ticket

Carmen Myrtis-Garcia was an award-winning women's studies professor. She was so inspired by the stories of women in history who overcame adversity that she founded a business leading retreats and workshops to help women set and achieve goals. Her professional life centered on planning, goals, and looking towards the future.

Carmen and her husband, Michael, had a long-range plan too. They were an unusual couple in some ways. Carmen was the planner and Michael the free-flowing man with a gift for laughter, art, and living in the moment. They met, fell in love quickly, and were engaged three weeks later. Neither believed in soulmates until they met each other.

In 1997, Carmen and Michael visited Caye Caulker, an island in Belize, and fell in love with it. They set a goal to move there in the future and open an art gallery. Then, on January 1, 2012, they arrived on the island with six suitcases after they'd divested themselves of all their other worldly possessions. This was their big dream and now it was their reality!

It wasn't easy. Now that they were stepping into their dream life, it was scary. "I learned that when a really big dream starts to come true, you assume you're going to be thrilled and it will be easy. Then it feels like you are standing on the edge of a cliff and your dream is waiting for you out there somewhere in the unknown. You have to take that leap of faith. Fear is there on the other side pulling you back into the comfort zone, and so you must decide: are you going to take that leap? Or are you going to stay where you are in that comfort zone?"

Carmen and Michael made the leap into the unknown. It took time and effort to find a home, to get the proper permits to open a business on the island, and to secure their residency. But, they did it, and they opened an art gallery. Michael and Carmen were so happy living on the island. They had time for friends, for art, for writing, and for living their dream.

That dream lasted for three years. Michael became terribly ill and eventually, after many months of pain and terrible illness, he had to be medically evacuated back to Colorado with Carmen by his side. He died shortly after of pancreatic cancer, shattering Carmen's dreams and their plans for the future.

It's been two years since Michael's passing and Carmen has learned much about herself and the flow of grief. Carmen is often afraid, but has learned to go forward anyway, even if it feels as if she is crawling on her hands and knees. She feels Michael with her. At times, her hand feels warm pressure, as if he is slipping it into his hand. There are constant little reminders that she is not alone.

One of the first things Carmen had to do was buy a car. She was afraid but found a car she loved and was astounded that she could qualify for financing on it. It seemed like a miracle and she burst into tears at the dealership. Soon after, Carmen discovered that she loves driving on country roads and began to take road trips on her way to her next visit to a friend or relative. "I had to learn to live with the deep loss and the vast unknown territory in front of me. I had so many decisions to make when I really just wanted to curl up and hide. I had to learn to move forward, even though I was afraid."

Carmen eventually returned to her island and began the process of closing the gallery and their home. She was afraid it would be overwhelming. After she moved out of their house, she did not feel complete, so she checked into a little hotel that she had visited many times with Michael. She was the only guest and requested the room they always used.

"I was afraid to enter that room, worrying that the pain would be too heavy and crush me. Instead, it felt comforting. I recall standing on the veranda, looking over the ocean and my beloved island and feeling immense gratitude. I had an amazing love story for nineteen and a half years. Michael and I made our big dream come true. We knew true happiness and deep love."

Carmen also learned much about the enduring quality of love. "I believe now that, when someone dies, they become even more alive. Michael is no longer in his body, but he is free. He's near me all the time, cheering me on, reminding me to laugh, and to trust that I will be okay."

Michael also taught Carmen to trust. He had a joyful faith, even in times of excruciating pain. "People were inspired by Michael. On the day before he died, he was laughing and celebrating life. He didn't get angry or pity himself, he just grew closer to God and to the people he loved. He used to say, 'No matter what happens with this disease, we win.' "

Carmen, the former long-range planner, now goes with the flow. She's learned to listen to her intuition and now asks herself what she really needs. She doesn't have a home base, but she travels and spends time with relatives and friends. She doesn't have a lot of money, but there is always enough.

"I used to love to plan out all of our vacations. Now, when I travel, I buy a one-way ticket. I stay until I feel like it is time to move on, whether that is a few days or several months. I'm just starting to be able to look ahead, even though I don't know what the future holds for me. That's okay. I have learned to walk through grief my own way and to not apologize. I'm different now. I don't know my future and that's okay. I've come to value freedom more than anything and trust that each one-way ticket or trip on the open road will lead me to exactly where I need to be."

Having a plan, just like having an answer, can bring great comfort, especially if your past has been full of chaos. Like Carmen, you've learned that even the best plans can't protect you from pain. When you lose what matters most to you, and survive it, you develop a special kind of confidence. It may be hard to describe, but you know it when you see it, both in the stories you've read in this book and in your own eyes.

The women of Scar Clan require freedom almost as much as they require air. Perhaps that need stems from the times when we felt powerless. So, whether you feel safest with a plan or you live each day from the seat of your pants, you deserve the freedom to make your own choices.

Looking in the Mirror

- When have you crawled forward, despite your fears?

- What might life be like for you if you did not plan it?

"Do one thing every day that scares you."
- Eleanor Roosevelt

Your Future from Your Deepest Fear

At fifteen, Jari Holland Buck was a typical Midwestern teen, except for one thing. She repeatedly dreamed of dying either by drowning or stabbing. She didn't talk about her disturbing dreams much; she just felt haunted by the idea that death was chasing her.

One day, it caught up with her. Her forty-three-year-old father died of an unexpected heart attack. Jari was very close to her father and she was devastated by his loss, and, as the eldest, she took over when her mother fell into a deep depression, taking care of her younger sister, managing the household and family finances, learning to drive and trying to hold her family together even though they had no money or nearby relatives.

During the next four years, Jari buried each of her four grandparents, her dog, her best friend, and the first boy she ever loved. Death was everywhere. Yet, she excelled academically, earned undergraduate and graduate degrees, and rose quickly within the corporate ranks. Later, she opened a successful consulting business, and she buried herself in her work and tried to hide her deep fear that she'd have to bury everyone she ever loved.

Eventually, Jari married Bill, an attorney who shared her distaste for death. He refused to make a will, sign any medical powers of attorney, or do any estate planning. Instead, he relied on exercise and healthy living. He described himself as "bullet proof."

One day, he collapsed at work and was admitted to the hospital with pancreatitis. He fully expected to be treated and discharged in about a week. Instead, a series of terrible complications developed.

Bill spent six-and-a-half-months in intensive care, primarily in a medically induced coma. His organs failed, he died and was revived four times, and he experienced thirteen episodes of sepsis. Jari closed her business, found someone to watch her dogs, and spent every day and night in the hospital with Bill for the entire eight-and-a-half-month experience. She shared, "I was so mad at death for robbing me of so many loved ones that I was determined to do everything I could so that death would not claim Bill."

Because Bill had so many medical issues, his case was handled by many specialists. One would prescribe a medication that would cause terrible side effects for another part of his body, then another would make the same mistake. No one was coordinating everything, so Jari stepped in. "I had to ask questions, be pushy, and make a nuisance of myself at times so that the doctors would listen, take me seriously, and then realize that I was their partner. I learned that is it vitally important for each patient to have a strong advocate to speak for them, especially when they can't speak for themselves."

Following her intuition, Jari took steps to make Bill more human to his caregivers. She posted photos of him healthy and looking fit, of their four dogs, and of their life together all around his room. She brought in his favorite magazines and some of his beloved model trains. A friend created a picture of an angel that Jari posted in Bill's direct line of sight in every hospital room he had. She asked friends for prayers and healing thoughts. At night, she held his hand and talked to him, whether he could respond to her or not.

After almost nine months in the hospital and rehab, Bill finally returned home. Unfortunately, he had significant brain damage and was no longer the man Jari married. With medical bills totaling more than a million dollars, Jari and Bill lost their home, Bill lost his career, and Jari's consulting business never recovered from her nine-month absence. Yet, he was alive! Death did not defeat Jari this time.

In the midst of all this stress, Jari realized that very few family members understand the vital importance of patient advocacy. While trying to put her business back together, coping with caring for Bill, and dealing with all the financial strain, Jari founded a nonprofit agency focused on training patient advocates. She also wrote a book, Hospital Stay Handbook: A Guide to Becoming a Patient Advocate for Your Loved Ones, published by Llewellyn Worldwide in 2007.

Today, Jari is a nationwide leader in patient advocacy, working with universities and organizations to train professional and family advocates. She also works with Shamanic practices to heal the land, animals, and people. She lost everything when Bill became ill – her financial security, the healthy vital man with whom she loved to travel and fish, her home, and most of her business clients. Yet, she also lost her fear of death. The more time she worked with patient advocacy, the more she realized that death was just a part of life and nothing to be feared.

She shared, "After all these years fearing death, it is now part of my profession. To redefine death not as a termination point but, rather, a transition to the next plane, has given me a wonderful vision of my future, whether near or far away. Death is no longer the enemy. I arrived at my life's work through death's door."

As I was conducting the interviews for this book, I noticed that many painful experiences opened doorways. Many of the women found new opportunities for service or careers after their scars healed. The process of experiencing deep pain taught them new skills and a profound compassion for others. Often, something good did come from their scarring, even if it didn't arrive for many years.

If you are in the midst of a painful experience, it may appear that you'll never smile again. Clichés like "There is a silver lining in every cloud," can make you want to scream. But hold on to that scream. The stories in this book prove that hope does exist. Healing will come. And with it, a newfound strength inside of you.

Looking in the Mirror

- What contributions have your scars made to your life?

- Which fears no longer influence you?

"I do not at all understand the mystery of grace - only that it meets us where we are but does not leave us where it found us."

- Anne Lamott

A Horse in Manhattan

Kathy Wood Dean grew up on the Lower East Side of New York with her two sisters and parents she calls "crazy wonderful." Her first scars came during her childhood. However, she prefers not to dwell on them and instead focuses on what she gained.

From an early age, she was very determined. The family had many challenges and little money, but they did spend the summers camping in army tents on a beautiful piece of property in upstate New York. She met a local girl who lived on a nearby farm and loved to go help with the animals.

When she was eleven, Kathy told her parents that she wanted a horse. To their credit, they did not tell her she was crazy or that it was impossible to have a horse in Manhattan. Instead, they said that if she really wanted a horse, she'd have to earn the money to buy one and care for it.

Kathy spent the next three years babysitting, doing odd jobs, and saving her pennies. She earned the money, bought her horse, and was very responsible with caring for it. That experience taught her that anything was possible if she would commit to it completely.

Over time, Kathy noticed that whenever she wanted something, she could make it happen if she was 100% committed to it. If she was only 99% committed, that one percent would trip her up every time. A horse taught Kathy that when we are fully committed, that commitment can be bigger than fears, insecurities, or doubts.

This insight into commitment carried Kathy through many rough patches in her life, including breast cancer and family struggles. She's observed that whenever you fully commit to something, all your doubts and fears will arise to try and stop you. There is a part of the psyche that wants us to stay the same, even if the thing that we commit to is something we desire with all our heart.

But each of us has a choice. We can back down and let go of our dream, or we can accept that those fears and doubts are coming so that we can heal them. If we can accept those painful feelings as evidence that we are growing, realize they are part of our evolution, and continue to maintain our commitment to our dream, they will lessen.

Kathy has always been attracted to spirituality. There was a beautiful church a few blocks from where she lived as a child, and her mother allowed her to attend it all by herself, even though no one else in her household went. As an adult, Kathy has continued to explore spirituality and her own development in diverse ways. Because she did not grow up with a prescribed spiritual path, she's explored many spiritual tools and techniques. Her intuition always guides her to what fits her needs.

"Trust is an essential part of success in every endeavor. When you can trust your commitment and your intuition, you will have the courage and strength to aim for what you want. It might not show up exactly how and when you pictured it, but it will appear in time."

Some members of her family are extremely scientific and analytical, including her twin sister, Leslie, who you will meet in another chapter. While Kathy can also be practical and analytical, she finds that following her intuition and heart gives her the balance she needs to navigate life. "I've found that intuition is simply opening your heart and listening. Whenever you need an answer, if you close your eyes, breathe, and listen, an answer will arrive. It always does."

Like everyone, Kathy's experienced pain, loss, and trauma. Each experience has shown her something new. Her breast cancer diagnosis was very shocking but something wonderful came from it. Kathy was astounded by all the love and support she received. She made a complete recovery and gained a true sense of all the people in her life who care for her.

"I believe that life begins outside of the picket fence," Kathy said. "Our brains may try to keep us safe and small, but life is about growth and requires risking and leaving our comfort zones. When we can balance our brains and our intuition, we can do amazing things."

Kathy's forward focus left a strong impression on me. I knew part of her family history and it was deeply painful and chaotic. She rarely mentioned it during our conversation, not because she is in denial, but because she's made peace with that part of her life. She's found the strength in her scars and used them to create a life that suits her perfectly. Bravo.

Looking in the Mirror

- What do you think of Kathy's suggestion that fear and doubt are evidence of growth?

- How do you balance your brain and intuition?

"I understood that I was inventing myself, and that I was doing this more in the way of a painter than in the way of a scientist. I could not count on precision or calculation; I could only count on intuition."

- Jamaica Kincaid

Courting Failure

My daughter-in-law, Allie, is a professor of Chemistry and is one of the most intelligent women I know. I fell in love with Allie the first time I met her when she was baking cookies and mending my son's jeans in his shabby grad-school house. Thankfully, Rob fell in love with her too. They both earned PhD's in Chemistry and are the parents of my darling Lucy, the muse behind this book.

I'm a recovering perfectionist because I was afraid of failing. If I didn't think I could win, I didn't play. Allie told me about how scientists view failure. It shifted my view and opened up many new possibilities for me.

A scientist courts failure. It's a good thing. You may have twelve ideas about a chemical reaction and ten of them fail. That's helpful information. In fact, scientists are not shy about publishing results of their failures, because it helps others avoid wasting time on experiments that will not work.

This was challenging for Allie. She's a bit of a perfectionist, like me, and initially took failures in the lab personally. As she progressed in her studies, she noticed a difference in her fellow lab mates. "There was a poster on the wall behind my desk. I learned it was there because the chemist who worked there before me got so angry that he punched a hole in the wall.

"Other students had to take a day off to mourn when they had a large project fail. My mentor was different. He had the ability to separate the results of his experiments from himself. To him, failure was nothing more than some molecules not reacting in the way we expected. He taught me to be more productive. When a reaction failed, I could just note the result and move on to another idea."

Allie did her much of her doctoral research on pharmaceutical chemistry. When new medications are created, ten to fifteen years of research is conducted, costing several billions of dollars. She learned that it is better to fail early in the process to avoid wasting time and resources on something that won't work. Fail early, fail cheap is a common motto in that industry. Knowing what doesn't work is an essential step in ensuring the safety and efficacy of a medication.

Allie also told me a story about my son, Rob. He went to a small state college on a football and academic scholarship. When he was accepted into one of the nation's top chemistry graduate programs, he was surrounded by students who'd graduated from Ivy League universities. His classmates had more research experience and had taken many classes that were not offered at Central Missouri State University, and, for the first time, he struggled academically. He decided that he wasn't going to quit, that if he had to leave the program it would be because he got fired. He was willing to work harder and catch up now that he was in the major leagues of chemistry.

Rob's willingness to try, even though he was behind everyone else, inspired Allie to be bolder in her career too. She shared, "Rob taught me how to get out of my own way and stop expecting to fail before I even began. Now I am willing to apply for grants or positions that seem out of reach. I learned to be afraid and do things anyway."

Allie also had to learn to stop being so hard on herself. "I used to get really mad at myself when I found a solution in the lab. Even though I succeeded, I would be upset that I had not found the answer more quickly."

The women of Scar Clan know failure intimately. We've encountered broken dreams, epic fails, and painful shortcomings. We can borrow some of Allie's wisdom by:

- Separating who we are from our results
- Celebrating failures as helpful
- Embracing the concept of failing early whenever possible
- Stop expecting to fail or avoiding something that seems too difficult
- When we do succeed, celebrating it instead of judging yourself for not succeeded more rapidly
- Celebrating your successes instead of judging yourself for not succeeding more rapidly

The next time you are afraid of failing, remember that failure is your teacher. It provides information about what didn't work, and that is just as valuable as success. Failing is temporary, and while it may be unpleasant, it's also an opportunity to grow.

Looking in the Mirror

- What failures do you want to celebrate?

- How did failure help you create a better life?

"It is impossible to live without failing at something, unless you live so cautiously that you might as well not have lived at all, in which case you have failed by default."

- J. K. Rowling

Love and Community

As a little girl, Stacey loved going to church. The ritual, the music and the environment filled her with a peace lacking in a home where painful scars occurred. Church was her sanctuary. She considered becoming a nun, but life took her in another direction, and she became a clinical social worker and pastoral counselor instead.

"For me, the two most important things have always been love and community. I've found that when I focus on love and am part of a community, I'm the happiest and the most connected."

When Stacey was in mid-life, she was diagnosed with two types of uterine cancer, one that was easily treated and another which was very aggressive. Her physician told her that her life expectancy would not exceed five years, because this particular type of cancer did not respond well to treatment. She was told to go home, call her children, and start putting her life in order.

Stacey and her wife, Joanna, were oddly unafraid. They called on their large community of friends and family and turned to their spiritual practices for support. "It was as if we were in a bubble of love for about six weeks. It was the only time in my life where I was free of judgment of myself and others. It seemed easy to be kind, to be loving, and to feel peace. It was as if I could see love in a limitless way and be that love." Stacey even bonded with her physician, a man who was from a very different faith practice than she was. Their doctrinal differences were unimportant, and they were able to pray as fellow believers.

Stacey had extensive abdominal surgery to remove any involved tissues to stop the spread of cancer. They were surrounded by people who prayed, chanted, and sang to support them. "Everything felt sacred. It was as if I was on holy ground during the entire experience, especially when post-surgical testing revealed no additional cancer. I was free!" This experience of deep peace and trust led Stacey and Joanna to change their lives and leave their beloved home, gardens, and possessions, in search of a simpler and healthier life in South America.

In order to stay in peace as much as possible, Stacey relies on her spiritual practices, as well as her contemplative and centering prayer. "I've learned to stop just talking about God and to start experiencing God with these practices. In contemplative prayer I focus on emptying myself of thoughts and just being with God in stillness. Centering prayer is a type of prayer where I sit quietly, and I welcome fear, pain, and judgment. Then I sit with it in the presence of God until it softens and falls away rather than me forcing it or fighting it."

In a way, the little girl who wanted to be a nun got her wish. Stacey leads and participates in retreats and spiritual groups and provides individualized counseling. Love and community are still the driving forces in her life. She has also learned to be more mindful of her own resources.

"Since my cancer, I have more grace and mercy for myself. I've learned that I can't offer to anyone else what I'm not willing or capable of offering to myself, and that, for me, has taught me that this journey is about practicing. I often miss the mark, fall down, and have to start over, but life is too hard, dark, and lonely when we can't give ourselves grace and mercy. When Jesus says to love our neighbors as we love ourselves, we miss the loving ourselves part. God calls me to be the healthiest, most loving, most grounded, most centered person I could be and, from there, if I am filled with grace, mercy, compassion, and love for myself, I can face some of my shadow. Then, as a result, I can also be of service to the world in my own neighborhood, in my own way."

I rarely consider giving grace and mercy to myself. While it is easy to be compassionate towards others, it is even easier to maintain a constant stream of complaints and criticisms in our own minds. I had a wise friend who once asked me if I would dare speak to her the way I spoke about myself.

While we can read numerous books about self-care, many of us still struggle to truly give ourselves the time and nurturing we deserve. Stacey is right – loving ourselves is one of the most important ways we can prepare ourselves for serving others.

Looking in the Mirror

- Do you find comfort in a regular practice of prayer or meditation?

- How do you offer yourself mercy and compassion?

"In this noisy, restless, bewildering age, there is a great need for quietness of spirit. Even in our communion with God we are so busy presenting our problems, asking for help, seeking relief, that we leave no moments of silence to listen for God's answers. By practice we can learn to submerge our spirits beneath the turbulent surface waves of life and reach that depth of our being where all is still, where no storms can reach us. Here only can we forget the material world and its demands on us."

- Alice Hegan Rice

SECTION 6

Contentment

The Gardener

It was her end
fierce pain crushing
consuming
leaving nothing behind
except
one small seed
planted long ago
by an old woman,
whispered promises
that she would always
rise.
That seed grew.
Tiny flowers of hope
mulched with time and choosing
harvesting contentment
in bigger baskets.
BraveHeart,
become the planter,
dropping blessings into
young ears
tired eyes
wounded hearts,
the furrows of the world
your verdant garden.

Contentment is not a popular term. I never paid much attention to it. When I heard contentment, I thought it meant being happy with what you had or settling for an unhappy existence. This triggered me. Did contentment mean I had to suck it up and pretend that everything was fine? I tried that for a long time and failed miserably.

Ten years ago, I attended a spiritual retreat. At the end of the retreat, the leader gave each of us a spiritual gift. Some received confidence, another was promised love, another was given professional success. I was the last in line to get a gift and I was eager to receive it. But when I was given the gift of contentment, I was disappointed. It felt as if I was awarded Miss Congeniality instead of Miss America.

Over the last few years, I realized how wrong I was to be disappointed in contentment. It is a rare treasure; I just didn't understand it yet.

There is a difference between happiness and contentment. In my view, happiness is momentary like bubbles or the peaks on a mountain. We have flashes of it and then settle into our regular routines. If we are lucky, we experience the feeling of happiness several times each day. I think of it like an exploding firework or a good orgasm, great when it is happening but eventually you have to get back to everyday life. Contentment is quieter and easier to miss if you are not paying attention.

Consider the ocean. Happiness rides on the waves, visible to the eyes, ebbing and flowing with the tides of life. Contentment is the deep throb that provides the base energy for those waves. It is a feeling of peace mixed with pleasure, the sensation that life is good and worth living. You can experience contentment when you are picking a flower from your garden, rocking a sleeping baby, or in the middle of a staff meeting when you look around the table and realize you enjoy solving problems and working on a team. Those flashes of everyday contentment are clues to what you long for, even if you are too busy to articulate it. Things like beauty, contribution, respect, coziness, order, simplicity, connection, challenge, and creativity.

Then, when you notice what your soul really wants, you can start to bring more of it into your life. In that way, contentment is something that you intentionally create for yourself. Contentment doesn't depend on externals. You can be content regardless of what's in your wallet, the size of your thighs, or even during a dull day at work. Contentment is a bit like a bank account. When you know what you need to feel content, you can build it into your life and add to your level of contentment.

For example, I never realized I longed for beauty. When I first moved to Ecuador, I was so busy trying to fit in and adjust to my new life that my house was left pretty stark with standard eggshell white walls. It was fine, but when I painted the walls in some of my favorite colors, I was astounded by the change in how I felt. My house turned into my home with a couple of cans of paint and some pretty houseplants. Then, when I hung a wind chime outside, I loved it even more.

For me, I feel deeply content when I am sitting on my front porch reading or writing, baking, grocery shopping, traveling, or having a deep conversation with a friend. I know it's strange, but I love to go to the open-air market for fresh produce or explore the shelves of a grocery store.

I have a friend who loves to sing. She is most content when she is singing, whether it's in her shower, at church, or along with the radio in her car. To add to her contentment bank, she joined a community choir. Other women find contentment in painting, swimming, volunteering, or running a company.

Contentment is a process, not a fleeting event. What you require to feel content may change over time and is influenced by your current life stage. When I was in my twenties, I wanted to have a family and felt deep contentment when I was with my children. Now that I am in my late fifties, I have more time to develop deep friendships with other women; something I was too busy for in the past.

It is possible for you build a life that gives you contentment. When you grow contentment, you will automatically find more bubbles of happiness appearing in your life at the same time. In fact, aiming for contentment is the most positive response to scarring. We can die from the pain of our experiences, or we can claw our way back to a life that matters to us. Our scars change us, strengthen us, and show us what we require for the deep peace of contentment and the base energy that says, "all is well," even when outward circumstances appear to negate that belief.

Safety is a pre-requisite for contentment. If you are in an unsafe situation, focus on moving toward safety. But keep your eyes open. You can still experience deep pleasure when you see raindrops on a flower, rub lotion onto your feet, or hear a birdsong. Those small moments of peace are grace notes, reminding you that contentment and peace are possible – and that you deserve it! Small things can engender great hope to sustain you during an illness or a moment in which you do not feel safe.

Once your basic needs for food, shelter, and safety are met, you can discover your own recipe for contentment. Your scars influence your contentment. If you were abused by another, you may need solitude to feel content. If your life was chaotic, you may crave a clean and tidy environment. If you were deprived of something such as comfort, opportunity, or acknowledgment, you will feel more content if you can find ways to add that missing ingredient into your life. For the women of Scar Clan, the journey to contentment can be long, as scars must heal and life can take time to smooth out. Yet, there will be moments when you realize that you are in the right place at the right time, that you have the capacity to move towards peace, and that there is good in this world, despite those who harmed you.

It is true what they say: Living well is the best revenge!

Looking in the Mirror

- How do you define contentment?

- Are you inspired to add something to your life to generate more contentment?

"There is no paycheck that can equal the feeling of contentment that comes from being the person you are meant to be."

- Oprah Winfrey

Feet in the Dirt

Dr. R. Hawk B. Lessard lives in a modest rental house in small town Oklahoma. Of Native American heritage, Hawk has spent a long time living and learning. She's had abundant wealth and she's been half a million dollars in debt. Her life has been a series of heartbreaks and miracles, and she believes that each day gives us a lesson to learn, whether that lesson comes with joy or sorrow.

About thirty years ago, Hawk became terribly ill. She lost her career, her home, and her savings; all the material supports she depended on were stripped away. She was so despondent that she asked Spirit to take her. When she finally fell into sleep, she heard a voice that told her she was to follow the path of a shamanic woman. She awoke saying, "No, no, no!"

Hawk went kicking and screaming down the spiritual path. However, wise women kept showing up and teaching her. One was Grandmother Turtle, a woman from Alaska who Hawk met in an online chat room. Hawk was living with friends in Michigan at the time after a very painful romantic breakup, and one day Grandmother Turtle called her and said that she was on her way, driving from Alaska to Michigan because she knew Hawk was in trouble. Before they ended the call, Grandmother said, "Little Daughter, I am here to tell you I love you. I'll be there in three days."

Hawk cried. When she was a child, she'd never heard those words from anyone. She grew up in very challenging circumstances, never felt protected, and was never encouraged. She honestly never believed anyone valued or believed in her. Grandmother Turtle was a virtual stranger who was willing to drive from Alaska to Michigan in the winter to come and help her. It all felt like a dream.

When Grandmother Turtle arrived, she asked Hawk where she sat in silence. Hawk took her out to the woods where they sat quietly together. Grandmother told her that the people she was staying with were killing her, and she would return in three days and Hawk should have her things packed. Hawk did not ask questions or say a word, but she believed Grandmother Turtle. Three days later, they left, and they drove across the Midwest until they arrived in Oklahoma. Grandmother Turtle told her to stay there and she began the long drive back to Alaska.

Hawk had never been to Oklahoma and knew no one there. However, she was tired of running. "I was a runner before that day. Whenever things got too hard or painful, I'd run, go to a new place and start over." But this time, something told her that she needed to stay in Oklahoma for a while.

One day, she was sitting outdoors with her bare feet in the soil. She decided that she would stay put until she learned about herself. She did not want to learn about what others had done to her or what she'd done to them – she wanted to learn about who she really was. A wave of peace washed over her in that moment, and twenty years later, Hawk is still there with her feet buried in the red Oklahoma dirt. She's learned to accept whatever comes along her path with gratitude and acceptance.

In 2001, Hawk was working a job she did not enjoy but felt she must keep for the money. On April 1st of that year, she made her final car payment, purchased four new tires and got her car detailed. Then, on her way home from work, her car was destroyed by a pickup and Hawk was severely injured.

When she woke from a coma, the doctor said she'd never walk again and would need a wheelchair. She said, "Bet me." Two weeks later she went to his office using two canes. He told her she would not get any better, and that she'd certainly never be able to ride a horse again. Again, she said, "Bet me." Eventually, after many trials and tribulations, she was able to walk unaided and ride her horse again. She still experiences pain every day, but does not let it stop her.

"Tough times hit at the strangest moments. We are not trained to overcome tragedy and usually don't know what to do. I've learned that all I can do is ride the tide. Sometimes we get hit with something so terribly painful that it takes our breath away, and at times like that, it is important to let your emotions out. Don't hide it. Don't tuck it away. If you bury those feelings, they will hurt you. And you must take care of you. You are the most precious thing you have."

Hawk turns to nature as a teacher and healer. She says that when she feels despair, she goes out to her yard, digs a hole, and pours of all her faith and sorrow into that hole. Some tears land there too. Then she plants some seeds in that hole so that something good can come of her sadness. This is a very healing process.

As a formerly wealthy, career woman, Hawk lives very differently today than she used to. She lives on a small Social Security check and is debt free. When her check arrives, she pays all of her bills, gets gasoline and groceries, and sometimes has just a few cents left over. "I give thanks for whatever is left over, even if it is only 64 cents. That's

64 cents more than I had yesterday." She used to have expensive clothing and beautiful shoes that cost hundreds of dollars. Today she has two pairs of shoes; one for daily wear and a pair of warm winter boots.

Yet, Hawk feels rich and blessed. She tends a large garden each year, growing enough produce that, when canned, lasts her for a year. She creates beautiful beaded jewelry, which she sells. She's found ways to live creatively and simply. There is always just enough money to last for the month, and when an unexpected expense crops up, so does an unexpected opportunity.

Almost ten years ago, Hawk realized that she wanted to help others more. She found ten old purses in her closet and started filling them with Lifesavers, wipes, crackers, and things she discovered at garage sales and second-hand shops. "If I found something useful for fifty cents or a dollar, I'd bring it home and put it in one of those bags. Each one of them was different." She put them in the back of her truck. One hot summer day, she saw a young woman walking down a deserted highway. She looked exhausted and hungry. Hawk offered her a ride and invited her to take one of the bags, a bottle of water, and the last five dollars Hawk had in her wallet. Over time, all ten bags were given away. Hawk always seemed to find a five-dollar bill in her wallet to give along with the bag.

Every year, Hawk creates more "blessing bags". Now she includes hygiene supplies, snacks, and a twenty-dollar bill. There are always Lifesavers in the bags because she wants recipients to know they are worth saving. There are no notes or written information in the bags. Her only request is that the recipient pay it forward to someone else when they can. Just like Grandmother Turtle came to help her, Hawk is led to homeless people who need a blessing bag.

"If I can help somebody, I'll jump at the chance every time. However, I've learned that it is important to read the signs and think about what you are doing. You have to look at why you are helping others. Are you doing it for your ego? Do you want others to put you on a pedestal? Can you give in a way that won't hurt or deplete you? If you can give from a place of gratitude for your blessings, with no attachment to getting thanked or even having anyone else know you are helping, giving can be one of the most beautiful things in your life. When you get your ego out of the way, life changes so much. I find helping others is as normal as breathing."

Today Hawk lives in peace and freedom. She remembers the days when her life was about the outside—money, possessions, and status. Today, she focuses on what's inside of her. She wants her legacy to be one of pure love, and she's told her landlady that, on the day she comes to Hawk's home and finds her dead, she wants to be cremated and her ashes thrown to the wind. Everything in her home is to be sold and the proceeds are to be used for a big party. That's all Hawk wants to leave behind her – memories of love, giving, and laughter.

Hawk's story illustrates the spiral nature of life and learning. Just when we heal from one scar, another may come along. We never get to the point where life is perfect and pain-free. We continue learning and growing until we are called to help others in some way. For Hawk, it was helping homeless people. For you, it may be that you are called to help a different group of people. Helping others is the natural response of a woman who has been wounded, because members of the Scar Clan understand pain and the power of friendship. We are uniquely qualified to aid others.

Looking in the Mirror

- How does nature heal you?

- What benefits do you reap from helping others?

"Blessed are those who give without remembering and take without forgetting."

- Elizabeth Bibesco

A Long Yes

In 1961, Betty left her home in rural Nebraska to become a missionary in Nigeria. She lived there for almost thirty years, met her husband, Wally, married him, and then raised five children in the mission field.

There were times of great joy and worry. When she was growing up, her parents taught her that God would always take care of her, and that proved true during times of civil war, illness, and natural disaster. Learning to live in a Nigerian village, to speak the language, and to form friendships was quite an adventure. The people in their village were very kind and taught Betty what she needed to know. She treasures her memories of sharing life and the Gospel there.

One of the most challenging experiences Betty encountered was when her son Michael was diagnosed with muscular dystrophy. His illness was severe, and the doctors did not expect him to live to adulthood. Betty recalls being so overwhelmed after the phone call with his diagnosis that she had to lay down on her bed and weep. She was terribly afraid until she had a vision of Christ and felt His comfort all around her. She didn't know what the future held, but she knew that God would be with her and her family always.

Michael is in his early fifties. Betty has devoted her life to caring for him, aided by her close-knit family. When Wally passed away, Betty and Michael moved to a university town in the United States. Michael's body is severely impaired, requiring a ventilator, electric wheelchair, and constant care. However, he has a brilliant mind. He attended university classes for many years. He also tutored other students when his health allowed.

Betty feels blessed. Her other children, their spouses, and her grandchildren help her with Michael's care, as well as a variety of caregivers. Betty and Michael have a loving and supportive church family as well. However, as his condition worsens, the physical aspects of his care become more challenging for Betty, who is now in her eighties, but God always provides the help they need.

A soft-spoken woman, Betty sees nothing extraordinary about herself, and gives God all the credit for her strength and endurance. "I'm a person who has always been a little fearful and doubted myself. I don't see anything remarkable in me, but God has given me the opportunity to serve in many ways."

Betty was a friend of my mother's, so I grew up knowing a bit about her from her letters and visits. Many years later, during a very dark period in my life, I happened to move to the city where Betty and Michael lived, and here was this woman with her seriously ill adult son who took the time to help me and my family. I was a single mother with many doubts about how I could take care of my children, but just watching Betty and her family care for Michael gave me courage. There was no pity or complaints, just a matter of fact approach to managing a complex medical situation.

Betty taught me much about motherhood. Her life centered around her faith and her family. Few mothers expect to be taking care of their children when they are grandmothers, but Betty manages to make it look natural. Because of her faith and trust in God's care, she was able to provide care for Michael in a way that honors his strengths and gave him the opportunity to pursue his own interests and learning. She doesn't know the future of her health or of Michael's, but she does know that God is constantly watching over them. When I think of a faithful mother, Betty is the first person who comes to mind.

It can be so easy to want to hurry our healing. We get weary. We can dream of the day when our problems are gone and our scars are healed. Betty's story honors every woman who lives with challenges that don't have an expiration date.

ng in the Mirror

)o you become frustrated when suffering lasts a long time?

* Where do you find the strength to hang on?

* Think of a woman you know who developed great endurance. How does her example inspire you?

"For I know the plans I have for you, declares the Lord. Plans to prosper you and not to harm you, plans to give you hope and a future."

- Jeremiah 29:11

Redefining Success

Dr. Lisa Van Allen was a powerhouse. She built a thriving business as a consultant and coach after a terrifying marriage to a mentally ill man. She was proud to be hired, to speak on stages, and to be valued. Along the way, Lisa met a wonderful man and remarried, delighted to have her personal life going as well as her business life.

One night, Lisa was attending a black-tie event in her favorite pair of high heels. She tripped and broke her ankle. It was a painful hassle, but she didn't think it would slow her down much.

Lisa was wrong. Three weeks after her surgery, she developed Complex Regional Pain Syndrome, (CRPS), a rare disease that has no cure. In a nutshell, her pain sensors became damaged and began to send messages to her brain that caused terrible pain, even though her ankle had healed without complications. The pain is so excruciating that it twists her foot and causes spasms. When it is at its worst, she can't have anything touch her foot without causing more pain, not even a sock or blanket. She is unable to put any weight on it at all and uses a knee walker.

CRPS is a mysterious and complex disease. It is considered to be the most painful disease known to man. Doctors and researchers don't know what causes it or how to fix it. Lisa has tried many different medications, surgeries and treatments, and has traveled around the country looking for relief, but her pain endures. CRPS is often called the Suicide Disease because it leads to deep depression and despair. It is easy to understand why people suffering from this constant, power-sucking pain would give up after years of no relief and little hope for improvement.

Most people who have CRPS take very strong opiate medications, and while these medications don't remove the pain, they do dull it. However, Lisa found that those medications were robbing her of her ability to think clearly so she stopped taking them. She's experimented with other therapies and treatments with varying results, and these days, she can sometimes divorce herself from her pain and put it on the back burner. However, at times it is so intense that she cannot speak.

Lisa spends most of her time in a recliner chair with her little dog, Daphne, who is a source of delight and joy. She's discovered a love and talent for sketching and art, and practices daily journaling. Her medical team at the world-famous Cleveland Clinic helps her manage her pain and explore new treatments as they become available. "Sometimes my doctors ask me how I am doing all this without medication. Drugs just didn't work for me. I got a lot of side effects with very little pain relief, so it is easier just to work through the pain."

Faith has always been a vital part of Lisa's life. She graduated from a Christian college and loved to study the Bible deeply, but since developing CRPS, she's stopped trying to study the Bible with her mind and learned to understand it with her heart, sometimes working on one word, in one Bible verse, at a time. She's found great value in mindfulness meditation and prayer. She has learned to listen for answers.

"I believe God has given me the grace to endure this illness because there is something I am supposed to do. For some reason, I've been gifted with the resilience to endure hardship. I don't know what my future holds, but I do know that I can still serve others and that is very important to me." Remarkably, Lisa has found ways to make peace with her situation and has used it to help others.

For the first year after her diagnosis, Lisa was not able to do any professional work. The pain was too intense, and she had to learn ways to manage it. She has to keep her foot elevated as much as possible. "I had to learn how to do things from my recliner with my foot in the air. It took a lot of creativity, but I even learned how to sew again. I have to do everything very slowly. It's become a metaphor. I have to really slow down to live this way and serve God." She's watched her business disintegrate and morph into something new. Lisa used to be so busy and reveled in her ability to work fast and be in demand. Life in the slow lane has taught her much about surrender.

Years ago, Lisa took a course in Spiritual Direction, a form of deep listening. During her first year with CRPS, she completed a refresher course and began to work as a Spiritual Director herself. "When I worked as a counselor, my focus was on healing the pain of the past. As a coach, I helped clients focus on their future goals. As a coach in Spiritual Direction, I now help people look at the present moment and consider where God is in the midst of their situation, and what can be learned.

"My job is just to listen. Sometimes I don't say much of anything for 45 minutes, and then just ask a question like, 'How is God showing up for you?' That deep level of listening, without speaking or interjecting my own thoughts, is a profound experience." Lisa has a few spiritual direction clients now. Interestingly, they all have some form of chronic pain.

"We are taught to take care of other people, to be the strong woman who has everything together. I was that woman, but I can't be her any longer. I had to give up control of my life and future to God, and that has been challenging."

Lisa encounters many who question why she has not been healed, why all the prayers on her behalf have not been answered. She has had dark moments where she lost all hope. At times, her foot twists in painful spasms so intense she wonders if her ankle will fracture again. She can't predict or control anything, except her beliefs.

"I've found that I can't be the leader of my family or my business like I used to be. I loved my work, especially speaking on stages and sharing ideas. I wrestled hard with God and kept asking why. It was not easy to yield to the sovereignty of God, but now that I have, I've found peace and contentment.

"God is always there for me. I don't know why I have CRPS, but I do know that it is my teacher and it has brought me blessings. I truly believe that God is good, even on bad days or when awful things happen."

Lisa had to redefine her measures of success. Instead of feeling successful because of how much money she made or how many clients she served, she now measures success by the sense of holiness she feels at moments in her life. "So many people of faith believe that we have to be stiff and serious about our spiritual practice. I believe that each of us encounters holiness in our own way. For example, my husband feels closest to God at a rock concert. My mother has holy moments in her garden. I connect with holiness when I am sewing or creating art. There is no single way to encounter God. Joy can be our guide."

Lisa includes mindfulness meditation, prayer, and creativity in her spiritual disciplines. She's worked to learn to be quiet and rest in God's presence. These practices refresh her soul each day. She also inserts her name into scripture verses. For example, instead of "My peace I give to you," she reads it as "Lisa, my peace I give to you." Inserting her name into the scriptures makes them feel very personal and alive.

"I've had to shift my thinking to God's economy. He doesn't value me any less because I'm not a sought-after consultant anymore. In fact, I am closer to God now than I was then, and that is important. I've started to ask myself what I need to feel nourished, enriched, content, and closer to God. Living a life of faith is not about rigid thinking, but about noticing joy. It can be there for all of us when we take the time to listen. My soul is prospering every day now, and that is more valuable to me than my bank account or client list."

Measurement is complicated. We've been taught that success lies in a certain income, job title, or marital status. Lisa, and other women who've healed from a painful experience, have gained a new measuring stick. Instead of defining their worth based on their bank accounts, they've learned to measure what truly matters: joy, contentment, love, and contribution.

Looking in the Mirror

- Have your scars caused you to change your definition of success?

- How do you feel about surrendering your life to the Divine?

"Great difficulties may be surmounted by patience and perseverance."

- Abigail Adams

Love Wins - Along with Laughter

Michele is a spiritual coach and a woman blessed with an enormous sense of humor. Her positive outlook and commitment to love are infectious. So when Michele was diagnosed with uterine cancer, she used all her spiritual and positive tools to come through the experience in a very inspirational way.

On the day that Michele got her diagnosis, she was already in the hospital. Some of her oldest friends came by and they started immediately planning her end of chemo party. The group was laughing so loudly that nurses came to shut the door. The nursing staff were worried that she had not been informed of her diagnosis— there was just too much hilarity in the room for someone who'd just learned they had a huge cancerous mass in their stomach.

Michele decided that she had a choice in how she experienced her cancer. She could wallow in fear or she could use the spiritual tools she shared with her clients. "My husband reminded me that this was a perfect time for me to walk my talk. I sincerely believe that there is a loving God who always has my back. I could choose love or fear, and I chose love."

Not everyone around Michele was so confident. Her in-laws asked her if she thought God was punishing her. There were painful moments during her surgery, radiation, and chemotherapy. "I remember thinking about my son, who was five at the time. It would have been easy for my mind to imagine that my mother-in-law would raise him, that I'd miss his life. Instead of those painful thoughts, I focused my mind on gratitude and seeing the humor in the situation.

"I believe that life can be hilarious, even when we encounter curve balls. I stopped watching movies and shows that had sick people in them and focused on laughing as much as possible. Some days I'd pray and ask God to send me funny things along the way. I also celebrated every possible thing. When we found out that 1 of my 13 lymph nodes were compromised, I high-fived my husband and we celebrated. That's like an A-, a wonderful passing grade. The doctor was a little startled, but he got used to us celebrating everything we could."

Michele was amazed at how much support she received. Friends, family, clients, and people all over the world prayed for her. When she came out of her hysterectomy surgery, her friends had hung a bag of margarita mix on her IV pole. Her doctor even laughed at that one. When she came home from her final chemotherapy session, friends had decorated her yard with balloons, streamers, and signs. There was champagne waiting in her driveway. Then a neighbor drove by and returned with his niece who was battling leukemia so that she could see a positive outcome. Michele loved talking with this young lady and encouraged her to start planning her end of treatment party as well.

Michele relied on prayer, meditation and gratitude to stay centered in love instead of fear. "I would spend time thanking every part of my body regularly. I'd thank my arm for being able to hug my son and all the cells for fighting so hard to be healthy. When the tears came, I let them fall. I tried to work with my body and never blame it for what was happening." She also had to become more comfortable receiving help and saying no. She loves to volunteer and help others, and it seemed strange to be the one receiving all the help. It was humbling to be surrounded by so much love.

When her nine months of treatment were over and she got a clean bill of health, Michele felt like she could breathe again. She's grateful for the people she met along the way. "This experience has shown me that we live on a small planet. We are all more connected than we realize. When I would encounter another person without hair or someone in the oncology department, our eyes would meet, and we would surround each other in love in just a few seconds. We didn't even have to speak."

Michele experienced tremendous growth during this experience. Her faith and gratitude grew exponentially. "I learned to turn all my worry over to God. If I really believe that He is love and is protecting me, then I have to live that way. I didn't stick my head in the sand and pretend that my cancer was nothing. It was serious. But, by turning it over to Him, I was able to listen to His guidance. I was led to amazing doctors and caregivers, and I was able to focus all my energies on love and laughter instead of fear. I believe love always wins, and it did."

It's easy to slide into depression when you are hurting or afraid. The women of Scar Clan, like Michele, do what they can to maintain a positive attitude. There will be days, and perhaps weeks, when it might be hard to see the light.

Create a stubborn commitment to laughter. Make it a priority to laugh at least once every day, even if you have to watch a silly sitcom. Each moment of joy or laughter helps you defeat fear and darkness.

Looking in the Mirror

- What can you do to bring more laughter into your life?

- Have you ever prayed for funny things to happen in your day?

- Think of a woman you know who developed great endurance. How does her example inspire you?

"Gratitude unlocks the fullness of life. It turns what we have into enough, and more. It turns denial into acceptance, chaos to order, confusion to clarity. It can turn a meal into a feast, a house into a home, a stranger into a friend."

- Melody Beattie

SECTION 7

Confidence

"Once you figure out what respect tastes like, it tastes better than attention."

– Pink

Measure Twice, Cut Once

In one month, I saw

A woman born without legs

dance, laughing and grooving

on tiny platforms

transformed to dancing shoes.

A singer, classically trained,

sharing her gift on stages

until cancer stole her ability to

carry a tune.

On the night of her birthday

she sang with the leader of the band

for the first time in three years.

It was a familiar ballad.

She sang it bravely and badly

by ordinary rules.

Those with eyes open

saw joyous abandon

a return to the deep love

thought lost.

How often I mis-measure life

thinking small is bad

large is good

preferring light over dark

easy over hard.

Until

I meet a dancer who doesn't need legs

and a singer without melody

and realize

beauty awaits everywhere

when I throw away the ruler.

Many of the women I interviewed spoke of the surprising confidence they attained after their wounding. Whether the scar occurred recently or long ago, surviving a deep wound carries an unexpected gift—confidence. For each challenge we overcome, each scar that we massage to healing, and each terror that we walk through, we gain trust in our own strength, our resilience, and our intuition.

Ruth Lee has been my friend, soul sister, and mentor for many years. She always told me that confidence comes from competence. I agree and would add that confidence also comes from surviving.

When women look back at the things that happened to them, many often say that they've already survived the worst of it, so why worry about the future? The ultimate strength of women is our ability to turn our scars into lovely new patterns of strength and confidence, and, as we age, that powerful beauty grows more luminous. The light of our souls shines more brightly, our wisdom is evident in our words and ways, and the joy in our laughter becomes less guarded. The women of Scar Clan are beautiful and have the confidence to make a difference. And once we've healed, we turn to the service of others.

The Dark Side of the Mountain

Frances J. Thomas was one of the most remarkable people I've ever met. A woman born with many strikes against her, she devoted her life to denying her limitations and serving others. I was blessed to be her co-worker, friend, and sister, although we looked very different on the outside. We used to joke about being ebony and ivory.

Frances was born in a city well known for its racial divisions. Her family lived in the ghetto, and when she was born, baby Frances was skinny, sickly, dark, and nearly blind. In the days before school desegregation and equitable public transportation, her family had few resources to cope with her medical issues. To makes things worse, Frances faced intense bullying while growing up, enduring teasing about her dark skin, thick glasses, poor vision, and poverty. She failed kindergarten because of her low vision and was sent to a school for children with mental retardation, even though she showed signs of being academically gifted.

However, her early struggles gave Frances a profoundly kind and accepting personality. Her parents taught her that she had a choice: she could be a victim, or she could use what she had to make something of her life.

In time, Frances proved that she could return to a traditional school setting. She earned top grades in high school and decided she would attend college and become a teacher, even though no one in her family had ever attended post-secondary. However, she could not see well enough to pass the physical exam required. In a series of miraculous events, Frances won a four-year academic scholarship to a local university. She became an optimist and thoroughly believed that she could face any challenge with prayer and hard work.

When she graduated with degrees in psychology and sociology, Frances prayed for a career where she could empower people. Once again, miracles occurred, and she was awarded a grant to earn her master's in social work (MSW) while working at a large community hospital. Somehow, she found the strength to work forty hours each week and carry twenty-one credit hours each semester. Because of her low vision, she could not drive, so Frances learned to study on the bus.

Frances attended a prestigious university as one of the few African American graduate students. One of her professors told her that she would never earn an A from him because of her race. He did not think African American women deserved to attend graduate school, but she refused to let that stand in her way. She earned her master's degree, and then served as a social worker for more than forty years while teaching at three universities.

However, her challenges never seemed to end. She had four experimental eye surgeries which required long recovery times. Her youngest son was born with a rare congenital heart defect and given eighteen months to live. As Frances said many times, she lived on the dark side of the mountain.

Frances relied on her faith and relentless optimism. She became a master of survival strategies and found ways to cope with each difficulty as it arose. After a risky eye surgery and the advent of featherweight eyeglasses, Frances was able to see well enough to earn a driver's license, and, after overcoming challenge after challenge, her son lived to age thirty-one as a dedicated husband and father in spite of his poor health.

She continued her career at the community hospital, moving up through the ranks of the social work department until she became a department head, and she worked there for thirty-three years and touched thousands of lives. Her final position was as a dedicated social worker for 2,000 employees, where she taught courses and provided hours of individual counseling. I had the great good fortune of teaching with her at that institution, which is where we became life-long friends.

Frances was famous for her pithy sayings. One of her best was "Thinking over Feeling." She believed that each person was capable of thinking through their challenges and creating plans to ward off problems before they arose. Her trademark hope and optimism empowered each person she encountered, whether that was a busy physician or a maintenance man.

When Frances was diagnosed with brain cancer, her ability to work from her strengths and rely on her faith served her well. Even as her physical capability dimmed, her light grew brighter.

I'll never forget the last time I saw her. She'd lost all of her hair and looked like a tiny, bald Yoda in her bed in a nursing home. She was glowing. Frances told me all about the staff members who stopped by her room to share their problems and get her advice. She was having fun helping them all, even as her body was shutting down. She was looking forward to seeing her Lord and her son as soon as she entered Heaven.

Frances was celebrated in a joyous funeral in a church filled with hundreds of people. There were tears, laughter, and a long stream of people who spoke about the impact she'd had on their lives, including me. She conquered the game of life, climbing beyond expectations in every area.

I keep a photo of Frances and me on my desk. I brought it to Ecuador as a reminder of how lucky I was to know a woman who never stopped growing and serving. Frances was fearless, buoyed by a stubborn faith. She liked to say that God kept the final score. I believe hers was an A+.

Frances, and any other woman in the Scar Clan, teach us to trust in our capacity to survive. That trust grows into confidence. We understand suffering, but more importantly, we have direct evidence of our resilience. Life may knock us down, but we will always get back up again.

Looking in the Mirror

- How have your scars fostered confidence?

- In what ways have your scars empowered you to serve others?

"We all hit rock bottom; sometimes, you bounce up fast, sometimes you crawl until you can straighten up and sometimes you have to lay there for a long time until you learn how to rise again."

- J. Autherine

Jump!

When Evi was in high school, some Peace Corps volunteers told her she didn't have to be trapped in her remote community in Albania and could be anything she wanted to be. They encouraged her to apply to study abroad.

Evi was passionate about science and wanted more opportunities to learn, so at eighteen she took the plunge and moved to the United States. Coming from a developing country, it was very difficult to get all the student visa paperwork completed, but once it was, she had to leave Albania in less than twelve hours. There was very little time for goodbyes to friends and family, which was extremely difficult for her.

Evi was from a small town in Albania. At home, she was accepted into the national medical school and her parents wanted her to become a doctor, but that was not her dream. She was the only student from her community to have ever been accepted into the national medical school, but Evi didn't want that life. Even though she loved her family and friends dearly, the only way that she could live the life she'd always dreamed of was to leave her home.

"I was so focused that I didn't have time to be scared. I wanted to change my future, and this was the only way." Her parents were terribly worried sending their daughter to a country they'd never seen. Moreover, they had no idea when Evi would be able to return.

When Evi arrived in the US, she spent the first six months with some distant cousins who helped her get a school job and enroll in a community college. She struggled to master English and pass the university English entrance requirements, but she was determined, and eventually she did. Evi was invited to join an honor society at the community college where she met many international students. These new friends became her support group and members of her American family. They all supported each other to reach their goals while navigating a new culture.

After a year, Evi got a scholarship to study at a four-year college in another state. Evi worked her way through school with scholarships and employment, often working two or three part-time jobs to sustain herself. After many years of study, she eventually earned her PhD. It was hard for her family to understand why her education was taking such a long time as it is almost impossible to earn a science- based PhD in Albania. In almost every aspect, there was a wide cultural gap.

Even as a little girl, her parents thought she'd ruin her eyes by studying so much. Her father was unable to complete high school, and while her mother had wanted to become a teacher, under the former communist rule she wasn't allowed to attend college. Evi's mother was passionate about education and encouraged all of her daughters to attend a university. The people in the village wondered when Evi was going to get married or come home. The idea of earning a doctorate in science was impossible for them to imagine.

Today Evi works for one of the most respected consulting firms in the United States. She was hired right out of graduate school, which is quite an accomplishment for a young woman from a small town in a remote area of Europe. Her journey was filled with focus and hard work, as well as the friendship of other international students. She had to make a new family in the United States, but never forgot her family in Albania.

One of her biggest challenges was feeling like a stranger to her younger sisters. Evi missed most of their growing up, both the challenging times and celebrations with family and friends. Now she struggles to speak Albanian when she talks with her family. "I dream in English now and don't understand some of the slang from home. It's really strange." She stayed connected to her family with phone calls, emails, and by sending money back so that her younger sisters could attend university. She had to make some hard decisions, foregoing travel and fun so that she could contribute to her family in Albania. But she was raised on the importance of helping her family, and those values have guided all of her choices. Now that her sisters are adults and doing well, she worries less, but still sends money home to her parents.

"I believe that if you really want something, you have to jump for it. Don't waste time being afraid, just follow your own heart and instincts. Other people will always have something to say about how you live your life, but you don't have to believe in their limited version of your future. It can be fulfilling to set a hard goal and master it. Just jump! It will all be worth it."

As someone who has left her country of origin, I could relate to Evi's courage to leave what's familiar in search of growth and opportunity. Each woman must risk in order to grow, and often that risk will include leaving the safety of what you know, whether that means moving to a new location, beginning a new career, or even starting a new wellness practice. It's painful to leave people and places behind, even if you are excited about the change. Like Evi, you may encounter those who disagree with your plans.

If you are preparing to make a big change in your life, give yourself some time to grieve the things you are leaving behind. Next, focus your vision on your future so that you have a clear mental picture of what you want. Only then will you be truly ready to make that exciting leap forward!

Looking in the Mirror

- Have you been limited by others' expectations of you?

- Is there something calling you to jump?

"There will be a few times in your life when all your instincts will tell you to do something, something that defies logic, upsets your plans, and may seem crazy to others. When that happens, you do it. Listen to your instincts and ignore everything else. Ignore logic, ignore the odds, ignore the complications, and just go for it."

- Judith McNaught

A Divine Safety Net

Shae Barnes is a successful businesswoman who has had her fair share of scars. The remarkable thing about Shae is that she has turned them into a radical kind of trust and partnership with God that covers every part of her life, especially her business.

In 2010, she was working full time in the technology industry and doing real estate investing on the side. Shae was ironing her clothes in a hotel room, getting ready to attend business training, when she heard "Go" loud and clear. It was the first time she'd ever felt like she'd heard a message from God, so she decided to say "yes" to Him and trust that all would be well. She called her boss and resigned that day, even though she wasn't sure what she was going to do.

Shae spent the next six months in what she calls faithless action. She was pushing hard, blogging, creating real estate deals, and doing everything she could to create entrepreneurial success. "I was pushing so hard and getting very few results, then I realized I forgot one important thing: I never asked God what I was supposed to do or what He had in mind for me. I just got the message to go and I went."

Then, a friend introduced her to a woman. They got on the phone and had a two-hour conversation. While they were speaking, the words Kingdom Driven Entrepreneur came up and Shae found herself saying that should be the name of a community, a movement, and a book.

The two women, who had never met in person, decided to write a book together. Soon the book was launched, and 500 people joined their online community. "It was hilarious because we had no idea what we were doing, just that we were supposed work together."

During this time, Shae attended a women's conference with a friend. There was a speaker talking about how God gave us eyes to see and ears to hear. The presenter asked people to listen for a divine message and stand when they heard something. Shae didn't hear a thing and was a little frustrated, asking, "Okay God, why can't I hear you?" Shortly thereafter, she fell on the floor and could not move.

"It was the strangest thing. Here I was in this big group of women and I'm on the floor with my nose on my friend's white high-heeled shoe. I can't move a muscle. I was so embarrassed and worried that they were going to call an ambulance. All of a sudden, I see a movie in my head. It's me as a little girl on a playground, doing the trust fall exercise where you fall backwards and people catch you. It was my turn and, just as I was falling, I put my arm back to brace myself. Then, I heard a voice saying, 'This is what you do to me. You don't trust me to catch you because you have no idea how much I love you.' " With that, Shae was able to move. Over the next few weeks she had other visions, all centered on how much God loved her. She committed to say yes to anything she was led to, trusting that it would be right.

From her new vantage point, as someone who was surrendering to God's leadership, Shae's life became a wild adventure. She was asked to write a book about sex with her husband. "I had no desire to write a book about sex and intimacy. That was the last thing I wanted to talk about publicly. But God gave us this information and I obeyed.

"I argued with God for months about that book. People love it! I've done interviews and spoken at churches and am terribly uncomfortable all the time, but I'm glad I trusted Him and wrote it even though I didn't want to."

Her next instruction was to create a business retreat for Kingdom Driven Entrepreneurs. Shae and her business partner obeyed and set up an event in Arizona. The only challenge was that they had no information on the agenda or the content.

"It was wild. We had people who purchased plane tickets and paid to come to an event without any information on the topic. God kept telling us to move forward and that part would be handled. Even on the morning of the event, I wasn't sure what we were going to do. It seemed crazy." In the opening session, Shae was inspired to share a story and then ask the participants if they held any unforgiveness towards a former business partner. People shared stories, cried, and cleared all sorts of pain around withholding forgiveness. The event was a success, even though the daily topics were revealed just moments before the presentations.

"I've really learned to listen and to trust. Now I know that there will be times when I am asked to do things and don't have all the details. That's okay. I know I'll be led exactly where I need to go. I am blessed to be in partnership with God, who knows everything from beginning to end. He loves me and everyone I encounter without measure.

"I used to hear those clichés about God qualifying the called and giving provisions for visions and thought that was just for church. Now I know that, in every part of my life, I have a divine safety net. Nothing will ever happen that is not part of God's loving plan for my life. I've finally learned to trust God completely. We have an agreement. I've asked that God continue to give me great stories to tell and they just keep coming."

If you are anything like me, you like to know the answers. I was that annoying kid in grade school who raced through her assignments so that she could be the first one to hand in her paper. When I have a problem, I research and look for answers. My ego is proud of my ability to know and solve.

However, there are some problems with no easy solutions. It can be a helpless feeling when you can't find a solution or impact change. In those moments, Scar Clan women remember that they have a choice between despair and trusting that a better day will arrive. Shae's willingness to not know all of the answers proves that it is possible to walk forward even when the future is hidden.

Looking in the Mirror

- How have you become more comfortable with not knowing the answers?

- What is your safety net?

Do not be anxious about anything, but in everything by prayer and supplication with thanksgiving let your requests be made known to God. And the peace of God, which surpasses all understanding, will guard your hearts and your minds in Christ Jesus.

- The Bible, Philippians 4:6-7

Authentic Beauty

Charlon Bobo is an artist of words and emotions. As an individual deeply aligned with her soul, she's worked hard to transform her profound childhood scars into strength and beauty. Her childhood, like many of ours, was marked by painful sexual abuse. It required many years to recover from her past and become a healthy, happy person.

Whenever I connect with Charlon, I'm amazed by the thought she brings to every part of her life. She doesn't just rush through her life unconsciously. She listens deeply, and follows her own guidance, even if it seems odd to others.

When I first met Charlon, she was bald and beautiful. Her makeup accentuated her amazing eyes and bright smile. I wondered if she'd been ill, but after I began reading her blog, I learned that her baldness was a choice. I became curious but didn't know her well enough to ask, then, after some years, her new online photos had hair! When I started this book, I asked if we could speak about beauty, and what we covered in our conversation became so much more than that.

There was a day when Charlon got an intuitive message to shave her head. She didn't know why. It was a like a tapping on her shoulder or a little girl tugging on the hem of her skirt. The idea would not leave her alone.

She went to a salon, and the hairstylist was horrified. At first, she gave her a very short cut, but when Charlon arrived home she realized it wasn't enough. So her husband buzzed off all her hair as she sat in her bathroom and watched the strands fall onto her floor. When he was finished, she went outdoors and felt an incredible sense of freedom. She raised her arms to the sky and said, "Here I am. Whatever you want me to do or be, I am willing."

She spent the next ten years bald. It was very interesting. People would come up to her and share stories of cancer and loss. Her baldness made her approachable in a new way. She would listen to the stories carefully and then say that she was fortunate enough to have a choice to be bald.

Charlon spent a lot of time thinking about beauty, and about who defines what is beautiful and what is not. She learned that the beauty and diet industry work incessantly to tell women that they are wrong. We are bombarded by airbrushed advertisements that plant an idea of unattainable perfection, just so we will buy a shampoo, an eyeliner, or try another diet plan.

During the time she was bald, Charlon had hundreds of conversations about beauty. She realized that she was lucky. Charlon's mother accepted her own beauty. Unlike some of the mothers of her friends, Charlon's mother never complained about her weight, age, or appearance. Charlon realized her mother was unusual in her self-acceptance. Most of the women Charlon encountered learned to dislike something about their appearance from their mothers, who may have learned similar attitudes from their own mothers. This practice of self-hatred was reinforced at every turn; on billboards, in magazines, and even in books where the beautiful heroine always wins the handsome man in the last chapter.

As women approached her and had these conversations about beauty, there were often tears and a few giggles. Being bald made her interesting to strangers and opened the door to many seemingly random encounters that felt like divine meetings.

Charlon realized that the definition of beauty is very narrow in most societies. Being without hair was one way to widen that lens and send the message that beauty is not about hair, skin color, weight, or apparel. It's about the light in your eyes, the warmth in your smile, and the depth of your love. She learned that all anyone really wants is to connect with others and with who we really are, and we wrongly believe that conforming to society's standards of beauty makes us more desirable and worthy. Then those who don't fit the mold – honestly, every woman – are urged to buy something, sending the message that only those who comply will be loved. It's a crazy and insidious message that runs as a subtext under all media and entertainment.

And suddenly, after about ten years, Charlon's intuition told her to stop shaving her head. She did and her hair grew back. She lost her unusual look, but not the power she gained during that ten-year period, where she came to the very edge of what she was willing to do to follow her inner guidance.

Because it was never about shaving her head. It was about being curious about what beauty really is and paying more attention to the subtle brainwashing women encounter. She gained power and self-acceptance by saying yes to making a radical change.

Yet, she doesn't recommend that everyone reading this book get clippers and start shaving. The point isn't the baldness; it is the willingness to take a risk that feels right to you.

Today, at age 52, Charlon still thinks deeply about beauty and power. She's aging, and curious about all the ways that older women hate their bodies, whether it be gray hair, wrinkles, dangling arms, or jiggly thighs. Who told us that beauty belongs only to the young? Why are women willing to cut out parts of their own bodies? She loves to experiment with cosmetics and hair color, not to conform to a prescribed image, but to play and explore. She's curious about what she might look like with purple hair. Her face is a canvas and she enjoys trying new things on that canvas not to cover up who she is, but to enhance her individuality.

Charlon recently had some new photos taken for her website. When she got the proofs back, she did not recognize herself and couldn't initially spot the problem. Her skin looked smooth, her makeup was just as she liked it, even her hair looked great. Then she realized the very prominent line she'd developed between her eyebrows was missing. She needed her wrinkle back!

"I earned that wrinkle. I have friends who did not get the opportunity to experience aging. My wrinkle is a symbol of survival, of strength, and of the effort I've put into life thus far. Instead of seeing it as something ugly to remove, I wear it as a badge of honor."

Charlon believes that intention is everything, even in the decisions we make about our appearance. If a woman wants to have plastic surgery, is she motivated by a curious desire to make a change or is she coming from a feeling of self-hatred? In her opinion, every woman is free to play and do whatever she likes with her clothing, style and appearance. When we accept ourselves as we are, whole and beautiful no matter what, we can experiment with anything that makes our hearts sing. It requires strong self-awareness to ensure that you are making your own choices out of love, kindness, and self-respect, instead of complying with indoctrination. And if you would feel better by making some changes to your appearance, nutrition, or fitness, do it wholeheartedly!

At the end of our conversation, Charlon and I talked about what our world would be like if all woman, everywhere, had an internal set point of love and acceptance, an unshakable foundational belief that she is worthy and beautiful down to her bones. We dreamed of the day when women are free to be who they are and how they wish to be, without self-hatred, doubt, or censure. We both believe that day is coming, and Charlon hopes to be there to celebrate it, with or without hair!

Abuse, especially during childhood, can leave women doubting their worth. So many of us heard messages that told us we were not enough, and these messages can wound just as deeply as a punch in the stomach. Our society bombards us with advertising that shows impossibly thin, perfect women, further triggering self-doubt in those of us who don't conform to traditional standards of beauty.

You have always been beautiful and worthy, just as you are today.

Looking in the Mirror

- What messages about beauty did you hear while you were growing up?

- How does your scarring impact your view of beauty?

"You can be the most beautiful person in the world and everybody sees light and rainbows when they look at you, but if you yourself don't know it, all of that doesn't even matter. Every second that you spend on doubting your worth, every moment that you use to criticize yourself, is a second of your life wasted, is a moment of your life thrown away. It's not like you have forever, so don't waste any of your seconds, don't throw even one of your moments away."

- C. JoyBell C.

The Power of Choice

Dr. Leslie Wood, PhD., is a phenomenal woman who changed the face of the marketing industry. She is a pioneer and an incredibly successful businesswoman. She's also the mother of my treasured daughter-in-law, Allie, and the grandmother of Lucy, the baby who inspired this book.

Before I met her, I was intimidated. Leslie seemed to have it all: a high-powered career, a doctorate, a beautiful family, and was organized enough to do all that plus make jam, sew wedding dresses, and help others. I was so nervous before the first time I met her that I got lost and missed the dinner.

When I did visit her home, I felt like I'd met my new sister. Leslie exuded a sense of strong confidence and infectious warmth, and instead of feeling intimidated, I was enchanted. Over the most scrumptious popovers I'd ever tasted, I realized that my son was not only marrying a wonderful woman but gaining remarkable in-laws as well, and by the end of the evening, we were family.

Leslie and her twin sister, Kathy, who you've met already, grew up in a creative and complicated family. Their unpredictable home was the site of both violence and love. There was frequent trauma and never enough money, but Leslie and her sisters always knew they were loved. She was very bright and got into a special public high school in New York for math and science, not realizing that it was an all-boys school just beginning to integrate.

Because Leslie could not predict her parents' behavior, she learned to rely on herself. That trust led to a deep confidence as she healed the scars of her past. "I know that I rub some people the wrong way. I'm very confident and have a high commitment to excellence. I learned as a child that it was always best to try to do the right thing. When I messed up, I'd take myself to the principal's office and confess. Things were always easier when I was the one to admit my mistakes and apologize first. I never want to do anything that would harm someone else."

When she went to college, she became overwhelmed during her first semester. She came home and went to bed for a few months and started thinking about choices. She realized that when she felt like a victim, it was painful, but when she made choices, she could cope with anything.

"There is great power in making choices. When I realized I could choose how I wanted to feel, what I wanted to do, or even small things like what I wanted to eat, I changed over time." Leslie began to heal the scars of her childhood, coming to realize that while her parents loved her, they were just nuts. There was no flaw in her that caused their unpredictable behavior.

Over time, Leslie developed a method that has served her well for many years. "I think about my life and what I really want. Then I write down three or four characteristics of what I want. It's essential to write it down and to not get lost in too many details. By writing down the essence of my desire and then giving it to God, the Universe, or a Higher Power, I am allowing for the best version of my dream to come to me. This method works every time. I always get what I need, even if the details might look a little bit different than what I imagined.

"For example, when I was going to get my first apartment, I wrote that I wanted high ceilings, large windows, more than one room, and something I could afford. My apartment had high ceilings and large windows that looked directly at a brick wall. I should have asked for light instead of windows!"

Leslie believes that the world is abundant and that every time a door closes, another opportunity arrives. "I've always been a bit of a Pollyanna, a person with an extra dose of gratitude. I go to bed every night and marvel at my amazing life. Even when I am the most stressed, if I focus on all the blessings in my life, my stress begins to lift. Gratitude and choice have been the keys to my life and success."

Because she had to put herself through school, Leslie amassed business knowledge along with her degrees. She worked in marketing and was one of the first to bring computers and mathematics into the industry. For her work in data analysis and research, she's been inducted into the Marketing Hall of Fame and has won many other accolades.

Yet, she faced a lot of anger during her career. There were other women in marketing, but she was one of the first who had the audacity to have children at the same time she was climbing the corporate ladder. "People told me I was squandering my chances, that I couldn't have a career and a family. But I did."

Leslie remembers a night when she was rushing around the house trying to get dinner on the table, complete with candles and linen napkins. Her oldest son, Bryan, was crawling around her feet. She realized that the most important thing was her child, not a gourmet dinner or a perfect table. "Jon and I talked about what we really wanted and decided that having time to enjoy our family was the most important thing to us. We didn't care about the laundry or cleaning the bathroom, so we hired someone to help with those tasks. We couldn't really afford it at the time, but decided it was an investment in our future, and it was."

Leslie has a knack for prioritizing. "I realized early on that I was never going to be perfect. I would make a lot of mistakes as a parent, as a professional, and as a person. All I could do was try my very best. Knowing that helped me let go of my guilt and fear. I knew that as long as my children knew they were loved, everything else would fall into place." When her children were little, she'd put them to bed with a reminder of all the people who loved them. "I believe that the more people who love a child, the better."

When I asked Leslie what she wanted to leave behind for our Lucy, she said, "There is incredible bounty in this world. When I was a little girl, I could not have imagined the bounty in my life today. But I did notice any little blessings that came along. I noticed, I was grateful, and I felt special. That gratitude brought even more blessings and magic into my life."

Leslie possesses the confidence that is a hallmark of the Scar Clan, especially when we reach mid-life. By the time we heal from our early years, establish an adult life, and learn to celebrate what we have more than what we lack, we have built an unbreakable confidence. As we age, we also realize that each of us has been wounded, and we are not alone. Instead of conforming to ideas that don't feel right, the women of Scar Clan have the courage to walk with gratitude in their own truth.

Looking in the Mirror

- Do you feel empowered when you make choices?

- How do your blessings help you feel special?

"Life is not easy for any of us. But what of that? We must have perseverance and above all confidence in ourselves. We must believe that we are gifted for something, and that this thing, at whatever cost, must be attained."

- Marie Curie

My Daughter, My Hero

Not every inspiring member of Scar Clan is an adult. Nakesha's daughter, Chrissy, is bright, happy, and wise beyond her years. She also has sickle cell anemia, a blood disorder that causes severe pain and medical complications. And Chrissy's had a lot of those. She was diagnosed at six months of age, and at the age of three, she had a stroke.

Chrissy had to have lots of therapy after her stroke to regain her speech and muscle control. She also had to have monthly blood transfusions. Because she was so young and small, these transfusions took many hours and were incredibly painful. Nakesha had to watch her daughter screaming in pain for hours every month and she couldn't do anything except pray. Nakesha's always been a person of faith and found that it was the only thing she could rely on.

When Chrissy was five, she had surgery on her brain to prevent complications. Things went awry while she was in recovery and her brain began to bleed, requiring another surgery. Nakesha was terrified that she'd lose Chrissy or that she'd have brain damage. "The only thing I could do was go to the chapel in the hospital. I got down on my knees and cried. I could not even form the words of prayer, but I knew that God would understand." After her second surgery, Chrissy was in a medically induced coma with a feeding tube. It took three months, but she was eventually discharged from the hospital without brain damage or a feeding tube. It seemed like a miracle.

Chrissy is a fighter. She's endured frequent pain and multiple hospitalizations. When I did this interview, she was in the hospital having fluid drained from her liver. Currently Sickle Cell Anemia has no cure, but Chrissy continues to beat the odds. Recently, her medication pump was removed because her heart function has improved. Yet, Chrissy has to fight with every sort of rare complication, some that even baffle her doctors. "I wonder sometimes why my daughter had to get this disease, why she has to suffer so much. She's a little girl who's been fighting this all of her life. It's not fair, but it is what God's given us. Really, I have to ask, why not us? I am amazed at Chrissy's resilience, her deep faith and trust in God, and her positive attitude. She's a hero to me and everyone who knows her."

Nakesha and Chrissy are a team, working together to conquer challenges and find joy in life. Chrissy is in middle school now and is remarkably well adjusted for someone who has had so many battles for her life. Nakesha clings to her favorite Bible verse, Hebrews 11:1: "Now faith is the substance of things hoped for and the evidence of things not seen."

They celebrate every positive outcome, every recovery, every moment they have together. "I believe that God is in control. He's given us so many healings and miracles. He made Chrissy and has a purpose for her life. He's given me a remarkable daughter who inspires me every day. We are blessed."

I can't imagine how difficult it must be for Nakesha to see her beloved daughter suffering and to have no hope of a medical cure. Chrissy's confidence and positive outlook inspire her mother and everyone she meets. Confidence doesn't come only to adults.

Looking in the Mirror

- How does your faith in the Divine, in goodness, or yourself, contribute to your confidence?

- Do you feel you were created for a purpose?

"Above all, be the heroine of your life, not the victim."

- Nora Ephron

Your Worth is Not What's on the Scale

Laura Fenamore was born into a large Italian Catholic family. The youngest of eight children, by the time Laura was born, her mother was being beaten daily by her father. Laura took to food for comfort and to replace the nurturing her mother was unable to give her. Home was a very dangerous place, but to Laura, food signified love. So, by the time she was in fourth grade, Laura was a very obese child. Then when she was eleven, her father hit one of her sisters so hard that she fell into a coma. The children were removed from the home and placed in foster care.

Things did not get better for Laura. She continued to use food as a way to feel safe in a dangerous environment. "As I grew up, I felt tortured. I turned to anything that would numb the pain— food, alcohol, drugs, sex." By the age of twenty-four, Laura was planning her suicide. Thankfully, she met someone who showed her she was worth saving, brought her back to God, and helped her get clean and sober.

Laura released one-hundred pounds and thought her life would be perfect. But that's when the real work of healing began. "I worked so hard to get clean and sober and release the weight. I honestly believed that when I got thin, all my problems would magically disappear." She turned to diet pills, laxatives, and bulimia. She lost weight but she still hated herself.

Laura spent the next years healing the emotional scars of her past. She had a message from God that she was going to heal herself and then teach other women how to heal as well. At the time, it seemed impossible, but that's precisely what happened.

In her mid-fifties now, Laura's maintained her healthy weight and built a life of love and happiness. It took a long time and a willingness to explore her many layers of pain and trauma, but now she works with women who want to heal their self-hatred and improve their health. "Women are culturally conditioned to believe that if they are not thin and beautiful, they have no power. At the same time, we are taught not to be too pretty, too smart, or too bold. Those mixed messages teach us to constantly compare ourselves to others. We constantly measure against other women. 'Is she prettier than me? Do I look better than she does?' It's torture and it creates internal chaos and pain."

It is easy to believe that we'll find happiness when we get the right body, the right job, or the right partner. However, those external things can't provide lasting peace. Laura believes that peace comes only from inside, from a connection to your soul, to faith, and to God. "The truth is that we are not our bodies. We are infinite spirits in finite bodies. As long as we measure our worth by how we think we look on the outside, we'll always judge other women as better or worse than we are. We should honor the body, take care of it, appreciate it. We are so much more than our outer appearance."

Laura begins her work with clients by helping women release their negative thinking and self-judgment. Some of her clients decide to release weight, but that is not the goal. Instead, Laura helps women focus on healing, both internally and externally. "My work begins with helping women respect, honor, and fall in love with the body that they have right now. It is a gift from God, just as it is." This is a difficult concept for many women. It can be painful to look in a mirror and see all the things we don't like. "We look at our reflections and hate what we see. We are at war with our own bodies. But we don't have to live that way."

It's also important for us to feel safe. Little girls are taught to fear, and often for very good reasons. "Society tells us that women are less than men, that we can be used, abused, and thrown away. It's important to wake up to those lies and learn to create safety in our lives."

Laura helps women see that they have taken responsibility for everything and everyone in their lives, but they haven't directed that same care and responsibility toward themselves. "Self-care is a practice, a process that we can master over time. It doesn't come from a pill, the right clothing or plastic surgery. It comes from a belief that we are worth it, no matter what size we wear."

Laura feels deep compassion for women who forget their value. She understands. Her healing journey has been a long process of remembering who she is – a soul in a body that was gifted to her by God. She's maintained her sobriety and health for almost thirty years now, though the journey has not been easy or without some stumbling along the way. The most important thing Laura's learned is that she is more than her waistline or her past scars, and that is true for every woman.

If you would like more information about Laura's work, I highly recommend that you visit her website at www.skinnyfatperfect.com.

Looking in the Mirror

- Do you suffer when you compare yourself to others?

- When you hear that you are more than your weight, appearance, or other physical attributes, what is the first thing that comes to mind?

"Confidence is the willingness to be as ridiculous, luminous, intelligent, and kind as you really are, without embarrassment."

- Susan Piver

Ignoring Your Expiration Date

When I put out a call on Facebook for women who had stories of faith and courage, several people said, "Oh, you have to talk to Wanda." So, I sent an email to Wanda, a delightful woman from Canada. As I write this today, it has been almost two years since I spoke with her, but her words have continued to encourage me to this day.

Wanda grew up a Christian home and relied on her faith even as a child. When her first marriage ended, she was devastated. Her faith supported her as she recovered, and after some time, she grew brave enough to remarry. She started a business with her second husband and was very happy, for a time. He had affairs. He would apologize and return to her, and Wanda would forgive him. This went on for twenty-three years until he began an affair with one of their employees.

Eventually he chose the other woman over Wanda and left the business. This was a very public humiliation. Everyone in the company knew what was happening, including all of their friends and family members, and now Wanda had to personally cope with all the rejection and shame while trying to run a business that was short on cash. She really didn't know how she was going to save the company and the jobs of their employees.

At that time, she learned about the Christian Business Owner's Association and found great strength there. She had a new community of other business owners who gave her advice and support from both a practical and religious perspective. The group would pray for each other, search scriptures for answers to their business problems, and lift each other up. In time, Wanda was able to turn her business around and return it to profitability.

During this time, she joined a new congregation that filled her with hope and joy. After about seven years, she met a man at church, fell in love and married. She was a little nervous about trying marriage for the third time, but this man shared her values and faith. Things were wonderful for eighteen months until Wanda discovered him molesting her grandchildren.

She was filled with unspeakable pain but she immediately took steps to remove his access to the the children, kicked him out of her home, then reported him to the police. It took two years, but eventually he was imprisoned for his actions. At the end of his sentence, he left Canada to return to the USA in violation of his parole and was eventually captured and imprisoned there.

You can only imagine the terrible sorrow this caused Wanda. Her family were so precious to her and the man she married caused harm to them.

Once again, Wanda was in the spotlight for a scandal. The case was covered in the newspapers and it seemed like everyone was talking about her. Wanda clung to her faith and her church family, and she slowly began to recover.

Then she was diagnosed with ovarian cancer. Wanda credits God with her being alive four years later. "He brought me the best doctors, treatments, and help, and I'm still here," she shared.

Wanda sold her business and went into retirement but found she did not want to stop helping people. She got training in Reflexology and Reiki and began using essential oils to support healing so that she could assist others going through physical challenges. She leads Bible studies and continues to be active in her church. Wanda was recently invited to join the board of directors of a Christian publisher. She told me, "I'm happy. I'm as happy as I'm going to get, and I still believe life is very good."

I have to tell you, by this time in the interview, my mouth was hanging open. How could one person endure all this and still have a positive view of life? I asked Wanda how she avoided becoming bitter, hopeless, and stuck in pain. She told me that her faith, family and friends sustain her through everything. Wanda believes that it is vitally important for women to remember that they are worthy, loved, and valuable. "In God's eyes, we are all cherished and adored, even if that is not currently happening in our lives."

Wanda also shared that she finds living in the moment is so much healthier than beating herself up about the past or worrying about the future. Doing that can be a struggle sometimes, but she's also learned that if she spends time each morning in prayer and meditation, her day goes more smoothly, and she can rest in the present moment. She calls it "chair time" and depends on that quiet time with God daily, both to pray and listen for answers.

I asked Wanda how she dealt with all the judgments and opinions of other people during the most tumultuous moments of her life. She laughed, "Oh yes, people understand one divorce, but three of them makes me a bit of a pariah. All I can do is thank God for my true friends who have always stood by me and ask for blessings for those who have left me behind. It hurt, but I can understand. Instead, I try to focus on those who support me and ask what I've learned from all these experiences in my life. I've learned so much."

Wanda learned to take responsibility for some of the decisions she'd made in her own life, to ask for and extend forgiveness to others, and recognized that God had always been with her, even in the pits of despair. "So often, we worry that God can't handle our pain, anger, or frustration. He can, and is with us just as closely in the dark times as when everything is easy. There is nothing too big for God."

When I asked Wanda if she had anything she'd like to share with women who are in challenging situations, she added that as women age, they become more in touch with their spirituality, which is a wonderful blessing. Over time, she's discovered the importance of a touch, a listening ear, and even singing a silly song to uplift herself and others. She said, "Everyone is going through some sort of pain, even if you can't see it on the outside. God told me to quit worrying about my expiration date and to do as much as I can to love and serve the people around me. I'm so blessed to spend time with my family, friends, and others. I'm going to keep learning, growing, and doing what I can to help others. That's the secret of a joyful heart, even if it took me a long time to see it."

The final bit of wisdom that Wanda shared with me concerned the importance of female friends. She told me about how her friends held her together during her trials, gave her inspiration, books, Bible verses, and brought meals. "Having a tight circle of girlfriends is essential in this life. When you have a group of women who will cry with you, laugh with you, and just hold your hand when there is nothing left to say, you are blessed. Create a circle like that and nourish it as often as possible. The support of girlfriends can get you through so much."

I felt as if I'd been given an incredible gift when I was speaking with Wanda. When I want to complain and throw a private party of self-pity and doubt, I remember her words and the warm, loving spirit that flowed behind them.

Looking in the Mirror

- Have you ever felt like a pariah?

- What do you feel about Wanda's suggestion to find joy in service?

"I don't have to figure my present circumstances out. I don't have to fill the silence left behind in another person's absence. I don't have to know all the whys and what-ifs. All I have to do is trust. So, in quiet humility and without personal agenda, I make the decision to let God sort it all out. I sit quietly in His presence and simply say, "God, I want Your truth to be the loudest voice in my life. Correct me. Comfort me. Come closer still. And I will trust. God, You are good at being God."

- Lysa TerKeurst

It's Your Turn

This book would not be complete without one additional story:

Yours

Imagine that you are sitting in a circle of women with kind eyes and open hearts. We want to hear what you survived, how you mended, and what you learned.

But, before you begin, let's talk about why telling your story is important.

What we hide, especially our stories of shame and scarring, can fester. We may think we're past that event, that it's been a long time and doesn't really matter any longer. We may have spent many hours reviewing that story with our therapist or best friend. So why do we need to go over that painful event one more time?

To be honest, when I was working on this book, I spent a few weeks writing all my scar stories. There were quite a few. I wrote, and cried, and revisited deep pain. It was wrenching, and then it was healing. I couldn't figure out why I suddenly felt better about things that happened in my past, but then I realized that the process changed me. I was different. Surprisingly, these Scar Clan stories helped me change how I viewed my past and allowed me to listen more effectively to other people's pain.

So now, as you tell your story, I ask you to write in a specific way, both to ensure that you feel safe and also so you can find the treasure your experience brought you.

You may write your story in the journal you downloaded at www. womenofscarclan.com/journal or on some loose paper. Personally, I prefer regular paper so that I can dispose of it safely. Your writing here is for your eyes only.

Make yourself a cup of tea and put on some music you love. I suggest using instrumental music so you are not distracted by the words. If you want some very peaceful music which you may not already know, Adrian Von Ziegler writes beautiful music. I love his relaxing Celtic music. There are hours of it available for free on YouTube. I am listening to him as I write this chapter.

Then, when you are safe and settled, write your Scar Clan story. Write it in full detail. It's okay if you cry. Those tears are healing.

When you are finished with your story, take a break. Go for a walk, pet your dog, or do anything that comforts you and grounds you in the present moment.

Then, when you feel safe and ready, grab a yellow highlighter. Review your story and mark all the places where you were brave and courageous.

Finally, ask yourself how that event contributed to your growth. You may find that it is a long list. Here are some examples to guide you:

- I got away

- I didn't give up

- I learned to have boundaries

- I asked for help

- I learned what I need to feel safe

- I grew closer to God/Spirit/The Divine

- I used this to help others

You are not condoning the event or the behavior of those who harmed you. You can't erase what happened to you. But you can celebrate how you transcended it.

"I love it when people who have been through Hell walk out of the flames carrying buckets of water for those still consumed by the flames."

- World Day of Metta on Facebook

SECTION 8

Mending a Broken World

The Quiet Game

She was a laughing girl
chastised for sound-
giggles, questions, conversations
while Teacher was talking.
After it happened
her words flew inward,
carefully hidden.
They thought she was shy,
a wonderful listener
lacking much to say.
That made her laugh.
If only they realized.
Playing the quiet game
measuring words by
the worth of the receiver,
proud of protecting.
One day, she stopped playing.
Words flew from her fingers and lips,
even from her hips as she danced.
The laughing girl became
the outspoken woman
stirring dissent, crying foul,
telling truths.
It was time
and
there was much to say.

173

I believe we survived our wounds for a reason — so that we can help others. Serving others is one of the most powerful ways to celebrate our courage and resilience. Whether you serve globally, locally, or within your own family, you have much to give.

Now that you have considered the stories in this book, as well as your own, I hope that you are inspired to do what you can to help others. Our world needs much mending, and the members of the Scar Clan are uniquely qualified to make a difference because of our empathy, courage, and hard-won wisdom. Whether you are interested in helping children, the environment, seniors, or the woman at work who looks scared all the time, you have the ability to make a positive contribution to the world. And you certainly don't need to be perfect or perfectly healed.

One of the most powerful ways we can help others is to listen for their greatness instead of their victimhood. People have always told me things that they don't often share with others. It started in the 5th grade at summer camp when a girl named Patty told me about having an incurable disease and often wanting to kill herself. This was heavy stuff for an eleven-year-old to process. There was nothing I could do but listen and offer her some encouragement, and we were pen pals for a while but eventually lost contact. Years later, I still wonder how her story ended.

Since then, people have trusted me with profound stories from their lives. I used to feel pressure to help them, solve their problems, or give them advice. I didn't know any better.

Now I know that when a sister is sharing the story of her scarring, the most important thing I can do is listen for her courage and reflect it back to her. Women in pain don't need pity, unwanted advice, or to hear your story of suffering, as if it's a competition to see who has the deepest wounds. In this initial tender moment, your friend only needs your presence, attention, and reminders of her strength and courage. If she wants more than that from you, she will ask.

Remember that honest sharing is a great gift, so when a woman shares her story with you the first time, honor that gift with attention, kind eyes, and a tissue when required. Avoid probing for details or derailing the conversation by speaking too much, and when the story is complete, resist your natural inclination to offer suggestions or an action plan. Instead, reflect back the courage that you observed. Witnessing and reflecting courage helps your sister feel safe after sharing with you, and recall that, while she did experience something terrible, she was brave enough to face it and to share it with you.

Use these questions to help you listen to and empower:

1. Where did she show courage?

2. How did she initiate change?

3. What creative ideas/solutions did she experiment with?

4. What did failure teach her?

5. What new confidence emerged from this journey?

You Can Do Something

In our current environment of problems which seem impossible to solve, it is easy to give up and believe that one woman can't fix a broken world.

That's a lie. When you follow your guidance, you can do great things. Whether you are called to mend a broken heart, run for political office, start a business, or create something beautiful, every step you take to make the world a kinder, gentler place contributes to a brighter future for everyone.

At this point in history, perhaps more than ever before, the Women of Scar Clan are needed. You may not have all the answers, or any answers at all. But what you do have is wisdom, strength, and courage. You earned those traits by surviving.

Will you join me in taking action to heal some of the pain and discord in our world? You may be called to act quietly, doing random acts of kindness. Others may be inspired to speak, write, or protest. You can hold a hand, plant a tree, or start a non-profit. Regardless of your path, wherever you look, something or someone needs mending, and each step you take to contribute to a better world matters, whether you believe that action is grand or insignificant. It all helps, and it all heals.

It can be overwhelming to think about all the problems we face and shut down. Instead, think about how you can make a difference. You may:

- Volunteer at a women's shelter

- Invite a coworker to lunch

- Join a community recycling program

- Knit blankets for abandoned babies

- Run for political office

- Mentor a young mother

- Teach English or reading skills to adults who struggle with literacy

- Join a group who prays and dances for peace

Please consider doing something, large or small, to help mend our world. Your courage, compassion, and wisdom are sorely needed. The beauty and strength of your scars gives you the heart and kindness to make a profound difference in our world.

When women heal, we take action to foster healing for others. It is a beautiful circle, and I'm proud to stand there beside you.

"Hold on dear friend, for this is not the end. You have traveled so far and you have worked so hard. Carry on with courage and do not give up. And not because things will be easy but because these seeds you are sowing matter, and they will grow in time, if you do not lose heart."
                                                    - Morgan Harper Nichols

Help the Little Book that Could Save a Life

You know someone who needs this book. It may be your sister, your niece, or the woman next door. Would you consider buying her a copy? My prayer is that this book will find its way into the hands of women who need hope, encouragement, and inspiration. Thank you for sharing it with those who need an extra reminder of their worth and power.

Thank you!

The publishing world is challenging for independent authors without lavish budgets or contacts who can open doors. If you found value in this book, and I pray you did, would you please go to Amazon.com and leave an honest review?

Your review of this book will help it get noticed by other women who are searching for inspiration and comfort. Reviews also generate interest from booksellers who might wish to carry this book in their store. I need your help in promoting this book. Posting a review on Amazon will take just few moments and will make a big difference.

Thank you!

Acknowledgements

I'm an avid reader, so when I get to this part of any book, I read every word of the acknowledgements section. I know how challenging it can be to create a book out of nothing except ideas, and that no writer is able to complete that creation alone. I've been blessed by many people during the writing of this book and am honored to thank them here.

This book would not have been written without the women who shared their stories. Their openness and vulnerability inspired and healed me as I heard their stories. Whether their personal story was shared in this book or kept private, each woman gave me a priceless gift when she shared her Scar Clan story. I bow before your strength and courage.

Dustin Bilyk from www.authorshand.com did a marvelous job with the editing of this book. His thoughtful comments and encouragement gave me courage and direction during the final months of writing. The book you are reading today is markedly better because of Dustin's careful editing.

My clients and students offered thoughtful comments and just the right words of encouragement during the writing of this book. I am profoundly blessed to work with the best people on the planet.

In Ecuador, I am blessed by wonderful friends and neighbors. Many contributed encouragement and support during this project. Whether you gave me just the right idea in a moment or have been supporting me all through this journey, a mountain of thanks to Cecelia

Lazo and the entire Lazo clan who have adopted me into their wonderful family, John Trotter, Magdalena and Daniel Herreshoff, Barbara Snow, Jari Holland Buck, Lorraine Askim, Marianne Schroeder, Susan Hart, Manya Arond-Thomas, Marty Castleberg and Torey Sedgwich.

The writer's community in Cuenca is rich and diverse. I give thanks for all the wonderful friends I've met there.

Lisa Juels and Ingeborg Majer are the godmothers of this book because they invited me to stay at their beach houses so that I could write to the sound of the waves when I was stuck.

Ruth Lee and Leni Onkka have been my spiritual mentors for more than ten years. My life is abundantly blessed by both of these dear friends.

Everywhere I've settled, I've been graced with wonderful, supportive friends. Thanks to all who listened, laughed, and lived with me in Minnesota, Kansas, Texas, and Missouri. Every time I think of you, I smile.

I was born into two strong families, the Buschena and the Stahlhut clans, and grew up on stories of faith and resilience, usually told in the kitchen while eating something delicious. I am forever grateful for that strong foundation built by my grandparents, aunts, uncles, cousins, and my beloved parents, Roland and Shirley. My godmother, Loretta Stahlhut, continues to inspire me as she lives faithfully in her mid-nineties. My four brothers, their wives, and children give me an anchor of home, even as I travel the world. I'm blessed to come from such good stock.

Special recognition goes to Shepherd Sands, the best listener I know, and a superb writer. Over lunch, cocktails, or the phone, you never were too busy to listen and encourage me. You deserve a medal and my abiding friendship.

Bob Higgins gave me laughter, encouragement, and a steady love that surprised us both. What a miracle to have found you at last!

My sons Rob, Tom, and Jake Hicklin, are the most important people in my world. I can't find adequate words to describe the love and happiness each of you provides. "I'll love you forever. I'll like you for always. As long as I'm living, my baby you'll be."

I was gifted with a wonderful step-daughter, Julie Klippel Word, who is, and always will be, precious to my heart.

And to my daughter-in-law, Allie, thank you for all the joy you've brought to our family and for the gift of our precious Lucy. I love you both with all my heart.

Finally, thank YOU for reading this book! We are connected, heart to heart, whether we meet in person or not. My prayer is that you feel stronger, prouder, and more valuable than when you opened the first pages of this book.

About the Author

Lynne Klippel fell in love with books before she could speak. Since then, she's been a teacher, a librarian, a healthcare administrator, a corporate trainer, and, beginning in 2003, a publisher, ghostwriter, and book shepherd for aspiring authors who want to write powerful and professional non-fiction books.

Lynne's had the good fortune to have helped more than 15,000 authors from six of the seven continents, publish more than 350 of their books, and pen 28 books of her own, both under her own name and as an in-demand ghostwriter.

She loves possibility, good conversations, laughter, cooking, and her adopted country of Ecuador, where she lives high on a mountainside with her rescue dogs and lots of books.

For more about her retreats, courses, and publishing services, visit lynneklippel.com.

Lynne enjoys connecting with readers and book clubs. If you'd like her to do a virtual visit to your book club, speak to your group, or answer a question, or answer a question, visit WomenofScarClan.com

Giving Back

At least ten percent of the profits of this book are donated to support women, including charities in Ecuador and around the world.

Free books are available to women's shelters, prison ministry programs, and other non-profits who work with women. To request a free copy of this book, please send a written request to

Lynne Klippel

427 N Tatnall #90946

Wilmington, DE 19801

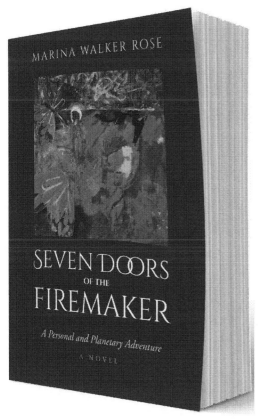

If you enjoyed *Women of Scar Clan*, you will also enjoy

Seven Doors of The Firemaker: A Personal and Planetary Adventure

By Marina Walker Rose, Ph.D.

"In every individual, in every moment, there exists the potential to become something greater, to evolve, to truly recover and know they are whole."

Irreverent, soulful, and epically transformational, *Seven Doors of The Firemaker* is the story of Helen Brower, an awkward, slightly adrift young woman who boards a bus in the rain and begins a rabbit hole adventure worthy of Alice and Dorothy. This book is much more than an entertaining story. It's an invitation to magic, healing, and understanding your journey in a new light. No matter what pain and trauma you've experienced, you'll find hope and power as you walk with Helen in an unforgettable and transformational journey.

"Paints an engrossing landscape …on a truly heart-moving, positive, hope-filled canvas. Here, the author blows gentle kisses to the boundless power of individual female self-determination as well as selfless women helping other women rise. My bottom line review? READ THIS BOOK. It could be a life changer." Amazon Reviewer

Learn more about *Seven Doors of the Firemaker* at Amazon.com

Made in the USA
San Bernardino, CA
24 February 2020

64882463R00104